REAL ESTATE

Your Blueprint to Move From Struggle to Success

(Real Estate Investing in Foreclosed Homes With
No Money Down)

Laurel Hazlett

Published by Oliver Leish

Laurel Hazlett

All Rights Reserved

Real Estate: Your Blueprint to Move From Struggle to Success (Real Estate Investing in Foreclosed Homes With No Money Down)

ISBN 978-1-77485-340-5

Legal & Disclaimer

The information contained in this book is not designed to replace or take the place of any form of medicine or professional medical advice. The information in this book has been provided for educational and entertainment purposes only.

The information contained in this book has been compiled from sources deemed reliable, and it is accurate to the best of the Author's knowledge; however, the Author cannot guarantee its accuracy and validity and cannot be held liable for any errors or omissions. Changes are periodically made to this book. You must consult your doctor or get professional medical advice before using any of the suggested remedies, techniques, or information in this book.

Table of Contents

Introduction

To accomplish this in the next chapter, we will discuss everything you need to know concerning ugly duckling property to enter the investment market correctly. Learn how to identify those ugly properties hidden in your neighborhood and are just need to be found, and how to distinguish the future swans apart from the lazy ducks. Also, you will learn what you can do to help finance your purchase, and how to turn it into a profit-making rental, and how to accomplish everything so that you are still making money when all is said and done.

There are many books about this topic that are available on the market thank you again for selecting this one! We have made every effort to ensure that it's filled with as much helpful information as is possible. Please have fun!

Chapter 1: Financial

It is important to begin with the basics. In order to enter the property market you will require money. These can be found in many kinds, but you must keep in mind that you have a variety of options and the more you take out, the lower risk and expense you'll face. Check out what you can afford in manner of cash-based purchases as cash is the most efficient way to go. Maybe you're able to form a an alliance with someone you trust, but should you choose to do so it, make sure that both of you are aware of their position in the hierarchy. If, for instance, you're going to be doing all the work physically, maybe they will be able to handle the administrative tasks, as the property brothers do. The biggest mistake you could make is to enter in a partnership with someone who has opposing thoughts than you do and is also looking to take command of the work. This could slow things down and result in tensions in the process. If your source of funding is to be cash , and you both agree to invest equal amounts and you are willing to work within certain limits, then it may be a good idea and you should create legal agreements that specify exactly what the conditions are.

There is a good chance that you'll need to borrow money to purchase a house. If that's the case you must know the maximum amount you can borrow and there may be an equity position in your current house that can be used to purchase other houses. Get a home valuation and discover. The bank will be willing to lend money on the collateral you hold in your home, but be aware. Be sure to keep the loan at a level that you can afford to ensure that you don't expose your home to risk. The loan you're getting in this instance will be secured by your home as collateral, which means that if you fail to pay the lender could seize your home away from you. Therefore, when you sign deals like this, be certain of the amount you can afford as you could get favorable terms , as contrast to getting the loan from scratch on an unidentified property. Discuss with your bank regarding rates of interest. Ask them about what your repayments will be and be specific about whether you are able to manage it.

If you're planning to take straight loans from a bank to purchase the property, it is important to be aware of whether short-term loans can be arranged at low rates. In addition, you have to look at different lenders to find out which ones are offering the most favorable deal. Tell them what you'd like the cash for and decide on conditions that are beneficial in terms of the length of the loan as well as the amount of monthly payments, and the penalty it is to take the mortgage out of your hands early. If you're working with a property which isn't too expensive, the bank might be willing to make this with the basis of a personal loan in contrast to one tied to a specific home However, the first thing you must determine the options available to you and determine your worth in the mortgage market in addition to the amount it will cost per month to keep that cash available for your home purchases.

The issue that people face when they are dealing with cash is that they don't think about what amount of repairs funds they'll require. If they loan $100,000, they then search for houses that cost $100,000, but this is a major error. You should look for smaller houses since you will not only be paying for the cost of the property, but there will be payments for the time the work is completed as well as the expense of repairs. If you're running out of cash, which is what many who attempt to flip houses fail, every month that your property is on the market will cost you money in fees as well as taxes, utilities and other charges. Therefore, the amount you take out should be sufficient to cover the costs and put the property on the market promptly.

Your marketing strategy will be crucial also because if didn't follow the steps in the chapters to follow, you may be set to lose money or discover that you own a home that isn't suited to a specific market and is in the market for a long period of time. Therefore, all pages in this guide are pertinent in the sense that the work needed done to a house will determine how much you are able to afford on the property. If the house you want to buy costs $100,000, however the repairs and renovations will cost $50,000, you will should have $150,000 and an emergency fund to cover items that might be discovered when you strip off the property to be renovated. Sometimes, you're lucky enough to realize that you don't have to draw from the contingency fund however, in the majority of cases there are things you didn't think would need to be completed and the contingency fund is the lifesaver.

Once you have established the amount you can take out, you'll be able set an upper limit on what you are able to purchase. Keep it in mind as if you embark on such a project with any type of debt hanging over your head , which you could not have anticipated the possibility of losing money. Contact your bank, your lender and potential partners to determine what financing you can get for you to purchase the house you want. This is your first step. As you become more proficient in flipping houses, you will realize that you are able to earn money from rental properties to pay for mortgages and that's when flipping property truly comes into its own. However, you've not yet reached the point of the game, and you must be aware of the financial state of your situation to ensure that you don't go into the market with deals that are too expensive in comparison to the amount you are able to borrow.

Chapter 2: Getting The Most Value

The sole reason why anyone is ever drawn to ugly duckling properties instead of turnkey properties that start making money from the beginning is because it's much simpler to find they are priced appropriate. In that regard, if you are hoping to have an abundance of rental swans that generate income, you'll need to know how you can locate the lowest price in terms of prices. Before you start, take a look at the options listed below.

MLS

The Multiple Listing Service is a database of all properties in the country that is advertised by an agent licensed to sell real estate. However, you don't have to be an agent to benefit from it but, as an investor new to real estate this website is a must be your first stops every day, and also the last website you check before going to bed at the end of the night. Competition on the website is very stifling, but this is because there are always new bargains popping up every single day. If you're looking to gain an advantage over the investors, locating the right real estate professional will let you think about other options too.

Take a chance If you are researching MLS in terms of statistics, you're most likely to get the most lucrative deals on Fridays and on Mondays due to the fact that there will be fewer people working on these days they are compared to other days during the work week. Real estate investing is a surprisingly flexible way to earn money. This means there's going to be more people than the average who take advantage of the fact that they can have a weekend that lasts three days. It's also generally harder to connect with realtors or the owners of potential properties on Fridays as well as Mondays due to the same reasons. If you put in the effort to keep looking at the properties being advertised on these days, you could be able to get new properties taken care of before other investors' weekend is even finished.

Maximize the time you have: When you get in touch with a MLS listing, you must to utilize the time to the maximum by bringing the contractor you hired or an inspector along with during the first visit. This will allow you to get the entire picture of the property as swiftly as you can, so that, if you do discover the right property, you are able to keep the process going as swiftly as you can. If, however, you are required to go back for another visit, it's important to finish the process on the spot during the initial visit. You never know when you're likely to be having difficulty contacting the agent once you're not in contact.

Be aware of the indicators of a good deal when you use your MLS it is essential to keep an eye for properties that appear on the site after having already been removed once. The most lucrative deals are made by buyers who will negotiate, and nobody will offer more that than after they've made an offer close to being accepted and then rejected at the last minute. They are typically seeking to finish the deal fast, so you can get a fantastic bargain. These kinds of offers are not a secret they are a lot of work, and speed is of the utmost significance if you want that you will be the only to make use of these listings. That means you need to be prepared with a pre-approved loan , or cash in hand and ready to close the deal as soon as you find the property.

In the end, it is crucial to remember that even with the plethora of listings being posted to the MLS each day, there are times when you'll be lucky, it's straightforward as that. Sometimes you'll stumble across an early-bird sale to snap it up, and other times the value of a home is less than it, in the majority of cases, it should be. Imagine the MLS as a lottery, If you don't participate, you'll never be a winner.

Motivated sellers

If you are looking to find properties that are cheap and especially when you're looking for properties that are ugly ducklings, then one of the most efficient ways to find properties that more than a dozen other investors aren't trying to get is to contact sellers prior to them making their way in the process. If a seller is represented by an agent in the real estate industry, the likelihood of negotiating a deal your favor diminish dramatically. That is why contacting individuals before they even decide to sell is so efficient. This method is most effective for those who have a reason for selling or other reason, have a urgent financial requirement that demands attention sooner instead of later. It is then possible to make an proposal that could solve the problem and everyone wins.

Direct mail campaigns Direct mail campaign: When it comes to finding motivated sellers in your region You'll be surprised at how effective an online search is. If you're in an average-sized city and you are capable of finding an organization that is willing to buy an inventory of people who have accumulated a large amount of debt for a low amount. Once you have this information all you have to do is take off your detective hat to find out the identity of anyone you have on your list. has property that is done by an easy visit at the office of the county's recorder. check the history of title for the county. This will give the names of every person who's owned property.

After you've compiled an individual who own a property and are in an outstanding debt enough to warrant the need to sell the property to pay over, then the following step you'll want to write is an informal letter. It is important to draft your letter to be universal enough that it could be used by every motivated seller you meet however, you should leave enough space to describe the particulars of the situation. In your letter, you're going to need to express your sorrow over the struggles the motivated seller is going through before stating the purpose of the letter, as well as the specifics of what you're offering. It is best to refrain from making an offer in your letter, but instead indicate your an interest in meeting with the seller you are interested in meeting in person to discuss the details of the deal.

Although every letter you mail out will not be a success in a real estate deal It only takes just a few minutes to make sure that you have plenty of rentals to select from. In the majority of cases, you can count on approximately a 3 percent return of sellers who are interested, which means that each 100 letters you send out , you can expect three motivated and interested sellers to contact you. The cost is around 40 cents for each letter which is 400 dollars and the cost of your initial list, you'll get a choice of rental properties that are starter real estate properties.

Courthouse steps up auction: Although it is not the norm throughout the country however, in many cases after a leanholder has closed on an asset and the whole process is unaffected and without a hitch, the next stage is to have the home sold at the location which may be or not contain the courthouse or any steps. The details on these kinds of auctions is usually accessible online through your county's website or within the Legal Notices Section of the local newspaper. The bidding process for these auctions typically begins with the amount each lienholder is due on the property being auctioned to ensure that, at the most, they could try to collect the money they owe back. When the value of loans in question is affordable, then this might be an ideal place to purchase a home in particular if you're not very picky in regards to the way it appears to be.

Unfortunately there is a lot of data available regarding the property being sold is usually very limited and is likely to differ between sales. Therefore, the inherent risk will be significantly more than it would normally be when buying a rental property. Higher risk means greater return, however, and you could get a home that is worth much more than you can manage with less volatile options. If you discover a price that is definitely worthwhile, you'll require money in your bank or a preapproved loan since you will be required to pay at the close time of the sale.

Buy foreclosures

The best advice for a lot of novice investors is to beware of properties at any stage of foreclosure process, it is because it's easy to proceed without having all the necessary information. If you do your research and be sure that you understand the details of what you're doing, it is a good option to acquire an unattractive property that is less expensive than what you'd otherwise have to pay. It is first and foremost that it is essential to comprehend the meaning of foreclosure since it has different meanings based of the setting.

In essence, foreclosure is the procedure by which the lienholder assumes control over the property in the loan when the borrower was unable to meet their commitment to the loan. What this means will differ based on the state the property is located in but each will include the time period when the lienholder cannot collect the loan and the borrower has no money to make payments, but legal action has not yet take place. As an investor in real estate you can choose from a variety of time periods that you can delay foreclosure to make sure you get the best real estate transaction possible during the sale at the courthouse as well as earlier in the pre-foreclosure stage.

Pre-foreclosure: This period of time before the legal process has officially started is called the pre-foreclosure period. Locating properties in this state may be time-consuming but the outcomes are worthy of the time and effort. In the beginning, you're going to have to study the default notices that lienholders filed in recent times. The information is available from the local clerk of court since it is a public information. The loans you find may not necessarily relate to real estate, but it's a good starting point.

If the results of your search are not satisfactory then the next location you should go to is the office of the county recorder as most of their data is only accessible via an open system, which means that it's the best location to go to if you require a deeper look. In this instance, you'll need to search for information about real estate or court records associated with notices of default. Also, you should find judgments against property owners , or concerns related to liens on properties.

Perhaps, you'll find the details you're seeking by checking any local newspaper that is slowing down. Legal notices in the newspaper might contain information pertaining to default notices in the event that the lienholder isn't able to serve the borrower with information about the legal actions being pursued. Addresses are often provided in such notices, which is a good opportunity to track down people who may be willing to sell prior to the foreclosure proceeding any further.

The people you locate by using this data are usually keen to negotiate since they know that allowing the process to progress through the foreclosure process can mean they are getting less than they normally would even with a bargaining offer. If you are attempting to approach a prospective seller in this scenario it is essential to have cash available or have access to a preapproved or hard cash loan. after you've got the homeowner in place, you are going to need to conclude the deal as fast as possible , before they've had time to consider their options and delay in hope of negotiating an even better deal. The aim is to give the most simple answer quick as you can, otherwise the value of the deal is likely to drop significantly.

Timing is everything.

If you want to get the most competitive price for an ugly duckling home it is likely that you will to prefer you to bring the first property investor at attend or be the last. As a rule an owner of a property can always expect to take the most reasonable offer they get. There are a myriad of circumstances that could change the truth, if you believe it to be the case, you are likely to be more likely to be right than not. Therefore, if you are looking to locate the top properties for the most affordable price, that means you're bound to be alert and looking for the next good investment in the event that you want that you will be at the perfect spot in the right place most of the time. One way to make sure that you're always first when you can is to create a precise plan of what you could be able to afford, regardless of the details and to never change. This will enable you to operate with precision and precision, as other investors let their emotions take over.

Another option, however the other option is to arrive late. This is especially beneficial for ugly duckling properties. The idea behind this method is to target specific properties that are put on the market for longer than could reasonably be anticipated. Be aware that if you're seeking properties with an actual fixer-upper potential, they could be the kind of properties that fall into your area of expertise. Although they may require some more extensive remodel than a typical one but the cheaper price is often compensated by the fact. Take a look at the numbers and then decide to make a change if needed.

Chapter 3: Signing The Agreement

Once the time is scheduled, you need to inspect the property, talk to the seller, and then make the deal. Be aware that it's an agreement until it's signed but it can be considered legally binding when it is deemed to have "seller's regret" afterward.

It is also possible to take precautions to ensure your safety prior to going into the premises since your security is the top concern.

If you are meeting to the vendor for the very first time attempt to meet him with a smile Smile at him and request that he lead you around the house to ensure that he is in charge of the situation at present. If the seller is reluctant to lead you around, considering that the home is messy and unorganized, you can put the seller at ease by saying, "This is nothing. The house you are looking at is one that I was in on the other day."

It is essential not to mention factors that lower the price, that would make the seller feel less secure as it's not the intention here. While the repair is obvious but you must continue to establish trust and a good two-way communication.

Scenario: Creative House Purchase

There are instances when the seller won't agree on a higher offer from an investor. This could be due to the seller doesn't like or believe in them due to their lack in establishing trust. This is a frequent mistake made by investors who are experienced sometimes.

As you've already guessed that small discussions are recommended in the brief tour of the property. It is crucial to involve the seller in conversation to collect information and this is the best way to establish trust. Try to be informal, yet in an professional manner. Since sellers will certainly trust you to be professional, as it shows that you know what you're doing.

In order to save yourself from your deals, it's important to deal with any situation with a calm positive, thoughtful, and validating manner but with a firm and calm manner. Professionalism and kindness are essential all during a conversation and it is through this that sellers will be able to overcome the fears or anxiety they have.

Certainly, sellers would expect this of you. That's why they will attempt to test you to determine if you've got positive qualities that will be the key to gain their trust, and allow you to manage the transaction.

It is possible to increase the possibility that the pre-screening process and building trust play a significant role in this. Additionally, you could allow sellers to see the flaws in your work to demonstrate humility and honesty while at the same time. In this way, you can inquire about the seller's motives by indirect means. If, for instance, the motivation of the seller is to relocate back to their home, you could ask them if they were raised in their hometown. However, you should never make a request that brings in negative responses. For instance, "So what was it about Las Vegas that you did not enjoy?"

This could lead buyers back to negative experiences that he might have had and could put him in the negative mental state which is not a good thing.

When you're finished touring the location You can now manage this situation. Ask to meet and discuss the agreement. Make sure you are near enough with the vendor while you read the contract in order to build the trust. The most important thing you must do prior to getting there is to ensure that you have filled in all details required in the agreement for real estate. The smallest details can make a difference to the sense of professionalism overall and creates a connection that the person has not consciously picked up.

When you're having the agreement in your hands, begin negotiations. When it comes to price, you should always begin lower than the amount you can pay. For example you want to pay 95K, however the seller is seeking a 100K price for the property. In this scenario, you could ask him "John We are within the same ballpark cost however we'll need to make it more affordable so it works for us both."

After that, you could be able to pause for a moment, and before taking the lead to ask the question "Let's take this. You're seeking 100K. I'm only able pay 90K if I look into the repairs I'll require. But I am able to increase it to 92K." Take a look at him following the question, and if you still don't agree with your offer , you can follow up with your next offer. "We are close, and in the same arena, price in terms of. Let's meet at the middle, at 95K." You can pause here for a second , and then request him to come back whether he would like to meet you at the midpoint. When the person agrees, then it's is it perfect.

Obtained Seller Approval

(Signing in the Agreement)

When the seller has was satisfied, you can read your page arrangement with him. Take his time to go through it , and inform him that you'll answer his questions following. While you are going through the agreement, be sure to highlight the key points in the agreement throughout.

If the seller is prepared to execute the agreement, make a note of the fact that he has already signed to signing the contract when the numbers worked for you both during the phone call prior to your visit. Perhaps on rare occasions you can say, "Now John, before I arrived you informed me that you could come up with an arrangement if you wanted to sign the contract." But in no way you'll declare, "But John, you assured me that you were going to accept the agreement."

After that, inform the seller the most important information in the contract such as the addresses of your mailing addresses and the seller. Also, present him with the price of the purchase, cash at the close, and the earnest money. You can also highlight that you've bought around 50 deals by putting 10 dollars in the contract. To get a legally binding contract, there are times when you require up to one percent earnest money. Naturally, you need to provide the reason for the 10 dollars. You could say, "You are going to get your money in about 5-7 days, so I've put the earnest money down in the agreement in order to sign it. This isn't really a problem since you'll receive all the money you need in just a just a few days."

The seller might not be interested in a deal if you do not make it clear that you are that is of serious interest.

New loan or financing

In the next step, you should talk to the seller that, under the new Loan or Financing section of the agreement, for conventional financing, it will take about three weeks to receive the cash. You might need to tell him, "I feel this in the event that my co-workers and I need to wait for more funds to arrive, though it has never been the case before. Once I've made an agreement, I will to stick to it regardless of what. I'm just asking my partner to provide me with an estimate of the repairs needed on the property.

If you don't, you can claim that you require the approval of your partner as he handles the financing. This will make the seller feel comfortable and allows you to get the loan you need. Make sure to note that the main goal now is to identify yourself as your new investment.

Closing Date

It is necessary to continue until the closing date in the contract. This is the specific date when the title company will complete all paperwork required as well as the transfer of title to the investor or you in your name. You can inform the seller you'll close the deal as fast as the title company completes all the paperwork in full and receives the cash payment from the bank of the seller.

The earliest date usually falls between 5 or 7 days. be aware that this is the one you will write in the contract under closing date. It is also possible to ask the seller for an appropriate closing date as well as explain that closing is the day when the property is ready and unoccupied.

If the seller asks you to discuss the 5-7-day closing, exactly what you have said to him, just tell him that the title could close this fast, but sometimes could take four days more in the event of a lot of activities. You could inform the seller that he won't have to wait for the funds as it will be available to the title company on the following day, and he will only have to wait for the company that holds title to conduct its search and to prepare the paperwork.

Investors should be aware that title companies are constantly busy and are not able to close as fast as they would like to.

Date of Possession

Possession Date is the day on which the property must be vacant and ready for move-in or for repairs to be completed. The seller must be removed completely from the property by the date specified. The majority of sellers take about 10 days to leave the property. However, some sellers prefer longer durations which is in accordance with the agreement. The possession date is usually given by the seller and, if it is acceptable for you, it should be included in this section of the contract in its entirety. But, it is important to keep in mind that you must to make sure that you set the Closing Date and Possession Dates the same in order to verify you know that your seller left the property following closing.

From this point, you will know what the seller's expectations and your risk tolerance is in the event that you decide to establish the closing date and possession date in a different way.

Possession against Closing Dates

Perhaps you've wondered the reason why you need to set the Closing as well as Possession dates separately. It's because it's possible to close within seven days, so there's a chance that the seller will not be able to leave in a shorter time. Additionally, closing as soon as possible could mean that your competition will not be able to take the sale by tempting sellers with a much more expensive prices when the title is transferred. After the title has been transferred in your name or that of your partner's name, it will be documented by the county assessor's office . This it means that the county recognizes that you are the new property owner, and it isn't able to be stolen from you.

Generally, title companies conduct a final checks under the name of the new owner to find any final Lis Pendants or liens that the seller might have been credit for at the time of closing. Lis pendants refer to lawsuits pending, which could occur when the same seller signs a new agreement with another buyer and then the buyer decides to file a suit. It is not often however if it does this happens, then the lien will definitely lock the property until resolved or removed by the buyer who is not the one that sued.

The third reason to set the date differently is to provide the seller with the cash to move out of the property. Then, you must be sure to keep at minimum equal to fifty percent equity of the seller in the title to prevent him from remaining on the property after the Possession date. This is not recommended for first-time investors, so it is important be aware of this too. Making use of hard money to close could cause the interest rate to rise quickly while waiting for sellers get out. You can however choose to charge the buyers on a daily basis to stay on the property for longer than the date of the agreed Possession.

Chapter 4: Assignment of Contracts

Overview

It is a good method to earn money with no risk, especially if you're just beginning in your business. Apply some of the basic marketing techniques to secure the best contract at an affordable cost, and then transfer the contract to a different investor at a cost.

The Positive

While this may seem simple and easy to do, don't undervalue the power of cash-generating of it. When you sign the contract, complete an contract assignment form, and then you receive a check. Done! Assignment fees of between $2,000 and $5,000 are typical in a well-written contract and up to $10,000 for a fantastic contract. You are paid once your buyer is able to take over the contract. If they fail to complete the transaction you'll still get the cash.

The Downside

Your profits will be restricted and you'll lose nothing If your offer isn't a success or you are unable to find buyers.

Success Strategy

Find your neighborhood real estate group and post ads on websites such as Craigslist. Find out what kinds of deals that investors in your region are looking for and whether they believe it is a good price. Begin marketing to sellers who are motivated to secure a contract that has a an extensive equity spread. Get the most business-oriented cards you possibly can from the people in the real estate organizations and include them in your e-mail list. Contact all "We Buy houses" notices in your local area and present your offer to them. You'll either get buyers for your offer or learn that you're in need of an offer that is better.

Strategy #11 Strategy #11: Assumptions

Overview

Also referred to "Assumable Loans", many of them are now accessible again. VA loans can be taken over at the current conditions, which means you'll get the house you want at a low interest rate , with no money down.

The Positive

You can avoid the requirement for down payments and can get a lower interest rate, which can increase the cash flow of an investment property that is long-term.

The Downside

It's not necessarily as simple as it appears. It is possible that you will be required to navigate a series of hoops. This could be as difficult when applying for a new loan. The loan will be reported on your credit in the same manner as the new loan, so be sure to combine this approach along with the "Credit Partner" strategy below (#18) to stay clear of using your personal credit.

Success Strategy

If you encounter an motivated seller with only a small amount of equity, but has it's a fixed rate loan that has an interest rate that is low check whether the loan can be assumed. If it's VA then it's probably. Contact your mortgage lender to find out which loans are assumable. This approach reduces the risk for the seller under using the "Subject-To" and "Lease Option" strategies below since they will not be held accountable for the loan once the buyer or you take over the loan.

If you do not want to own the property for yourself, but you have a buyer who can be able to take it on (but they do not have a downpayment) You may be able to let them assume the loan in the first place and carry over the equity spread into the second mortgage, which will be paid every month. Instead of receiving cash profits you'd get a note that would pay your earnings to you every month, in addition to interest as a reward for creating the contract between the seller and the buyer.

Strategy #12 Option #12: Lease

Overview

Lease options are actually an excellent option to "control" the majority of properties but without "owning" the property. A lease option gives you the option of purchasing an asset at a set cost, and within a predetermined time frame. You can choose not to purchase the property in the event that the market doesn't provide enough profit for you, or if do not have a buyer. If you aren't satisfied with the offer, you can simply return the property back at time you're done and your credit score is not affected.

The Positive

As low as $0 and up to just a few thousand it is possible to control your home for less than a down payment but still have the option to sell the house at a greater price at any point during the time frame of your Option. This is a fantastic opportunity to raise very small sums of money, and possibly earn an enormous profit.

The Downside

While you may be able to get a lease-option for very minimal or no cost however, some sellers may require some thousand dollars in order to allow you to manage the property for a set price for a specific time period. If you don't purchase the property in the future then you'll lose the option cash (which you might have borrowed, and are now owed by somebody else).

Success Strategy

"Lease-Option Sandwiches" are a excellent way to construct an investment portfolio that require no money or credit involved and generate an income stream that is passive, and potentially a huge profit spread in only a couple of years, and all with low risk.

Begin your campaign by marketing your home to "Rent-To-Own" tenants who have at least $3,000-$10,000 to pay for buying their new home. They could be self-employed, do not have enough money to make the full amount of a down payment, or may have a few credit issues. Start looking for interested sellers who would be willing to let their house or allow someone else to help with mortgage payments. You can sign a lease-option contract to get the lowest monthly payment , the amount of down payment (if there is one) and purchase price, but with the longest time frame (2 or 5 years is you prefer). Then, you can get a bigger deposit from the Rent To Own (Lease-Option) tenant and a higher amount of rent, as well as then charge the higher price for your option and you should make the contract for shorter terms (preferably one year). Create a spread to profits in multiple places and provide time for the possibility of a tenant's departure in case the first tenant isn't able to purchase the home. It is possible to make a lot of cash before the option runs out even if the property doesn't sell, and you decide to give the property back to the original owners.

Chapter 5: Website Names

For starting out, the first step is to select the right name for your website. In the event that you're in a completely new resort, town city, or suburb It is likely to be a challenge to come up with a great name for your website in the event that you don't already have one or one that comes naturally if someone was searching for a property in your region. Don't panic. It's not too big of an issue as you'll be able to see when we walk through the steps of this method. You should try to get as perfect name for a real estate website as you can. A name that is relevant to your local area and that you could input into your search box if looking for properties in your local area. For example, NewYorkRealEstate.com or LosAngelesDreamHomes.com or TampaHomeSearcher.com or RealEstateInMaui.com. There are numerous combinations you can make.

One quick side note: do not use your name as a website. If you are selling real estate in New York, your real estate website should not be BobSmithRealEstate.com, which you will understand soon. If it is your site then you must purchase a new name for the purpose of this system and get it redirect to your primary website.

As I said, finding the right name isn't all that important, however you should try to be pertinent to your local area in order to be able to discover later in the examples in the following, when your website shows on the page of ads on Google or Yahoo the website's name will be displayed. If someone goes onto Google and types in New York Real Estate, and your ad comes up in the results but it says NewJerseyHomeSearcher.com or BobSmithRealEstate.com, they are less likely to click on it. This will become more clear as we progress. Also, if you can get an impressive name, it can help with organic search results, but it isn't necessary to create leads using my method.

I always attempt to find an .com name whenever I can, but should you cannot get the .com version isn't accessible, it's essential to choose an appropriate name for the region so that when your ad appears in search results, it is logical. So if you can get a really great name, like NewYorkRealEstate.net instead of .com, go for it.

Search Keywords

Search terms are terms you'll need to buy to ensure your website appears in the initial page of search engines whenever potential visitors search for those keywords. Like I said the website you have created is likely to not show to the top page of an search engine naturally. However, if it happens, you're likely to be spending a significant amount of money to ensure that this occurs. It is something you have to be in the loop or have someone else perform, since in the event that you do not then your website will slide lower in the rankings. Search terms provide an easier and affordable method to ensure that your site is listed in the very first page of search engines when potential customers are searching for homes in your region.

Just like choosing the right name for your website, do the process of thinking about the possible combinations you could choose if you were to search for properties in your local area. Contrary to the name of your website that you select the name you think is the most appropriate to your region You can use as many search terms as you like. For example, if your website was www.NewYorkRealEstate.net, you may want to buy the search terms, Real Estate in New York, New York Property For Sale, New York Apartments For Sale, etc. When you've got all the terms you think are most appropriate There are a variety of methods to purchase these terms to ensure that your advertisement is displayed in page on the search results.

My preferred method is to buy from an organization that is focused on making sure that your site shows at the very top of page whenever someone type into any of the search phrases. This is not the same as AdWords or Pay-Per-Clicks . I prefer this option, in part due to the fact that you are paying a monthly , flat rate and it's less labor-intensive. The company I work with for this is World Wide Media Group and I've included their contact info at the end of this article. There are a lot of firms that can do this. I like them and have had excellent success with them.

Next step most crucial, and I call this "The Lead Capture Page."

It is essential to have a compelling headline and an appealing advertisement that will get the potential customer to click on your search result above the others.

For instance, if prospects type into "Gotham home search" Results pop up, and your ad might need to appear something like this:

Gotham Home Search

www.GothamHomeSearcher.com

Are you looking for Property? Start Your Find Here

or

Gotham Home Search

www.GothamHomeSearcher.com

Search for Every Home located in Gotham Free!

or

Gotham Home Search

www.GothamHomeSearcher.com

Explore a huge selection of homes in a few clicks!

You're probably getting the picture and you understand what you market far better than me. So anything you can put into an easy and concise way that can convince someone to go to your site before they click this is the approach you should be using. This is the reason the reason it is crucial to make an effort to get a website name that fits the area you are in, as we mentioned earlier. Because the name of the website is shown in the advertisement it is important to ensure it's a good fit. If someone is looking for Homes in Gotham and they see GothamHomeSearcher.com, they are more likely to click that ad over BobSmithRealEstate.com.

If a potential buyer clicks your advertisement, they'll be taken to the Lead Capture Page, not the home page of your broker or personal website. The page must be easy to navigate with a heading that reads something similar to Gotham Home Searcher, and the bottom of the page should be able start their search. No broker's name, there are no additional tabs and that's all there is.

WELCOME TO
GOTHAM HOME SEARCHER

Begin your FREE search here for all available properties in the Gotham Area, no obligation, no hassle, just good information.

Type of Home:
City/Area:
or Zip Code:

NEXT>>>>

Here's a basic picture for what your page could look like after you have people click your ad. I'm sure that your web designer will be able to make it better but it must be this easy.

I do not want you to violate any laws or go over the ethical boundaries and so, adhere to the rules you must follow. If you require

46

the name of your broker, write it in tiny print at the bottom. It could be something like this page was provided to you from Blank Real Estate Corporation John Smith, broker, but it is not required to be the very first page that a potential client encounters when they visit the broker's home page. Remove the ego from it. The aim is to take an lead.

The person who has clicked on your advertisement will be taken to an search page that will allow them to feel secure that they can search for properties within the area they're interested in. They'll begin filling in the details that follows, which is the final thing that's crucial.

Chapter 6: Selling A Home In A Short Sale

As we've mentioned before, certain transactions require representation from an agent for real estate. Short sales are a type of transactions that fall into the same category. The term "short sale" refers to a type of real estate transaction in which a bank accepts a selling a property at lesser than what is due to them.

A short sale is more appealing in the eyes of your lending institution than foreclosure, because to banks it's less expensive and easier for you to locate buyers as opposed to having to locate one. A lender pays hefty legal fees when they foreclose on a home.

Once they have a home The bank accumulates maintenance charges, upkeep costs as well as property tax, utility bills, fee for asset managers and so the list goes on... as the expenses continue to grow until the house is sold.

Agent representation is usually required by banks to guarantee an arm's-length transaction. For short sales an arm's length deal is one in which the purchaser and seller do not have any connection to one another , whether through marriage, blood or any other business agreement.

The seller's lender(s) will have the parties sign an Affidavit for Arm's Length transaction. The document demonstrates that the parties are independent, and each is acting in their best interest to receive the most fair market price. Common problems with "arm's length" conditions for Short Sales include: 1.) The lenders who finance Short Sales will not permit an agent of real estate to market their own property as a possibility for a short sale.) they will prohibit an agent who is connected to the seller to advertise the property. Furthermore buyers and seller should not be in any other relationship, apart from buyer and seller. They are also ensuring that the parties aren't business partners or family members and that the sale will result in the an actual market value. market value.

How can you make sure that a property you are selling completed and approved? To successfully sell a home in a short sale your homeowner's lender(s) must agree to the sale and accept all the conditions.

It's crucial to locate an agent who is experienced in short sales to succeed. An experienced agent is likely to be familiar with the lending institution, their policies and the required paperwork. It is best to find someone who has these details prior to the time of the transaction so that the transaction doesn't get delayed.

Because the lender is going to pay agents' commissions, there's no reason to list the home by someone who isn't experienced in short sales. Since the lender will be paying for it, the homeowner must go out and locate a person with lots of expertise!

Certain homeowners will take the initiative and put their home on the market ahead of any adverse action that are initiated by the lending institution. When I refer to adverse actions, I'm referring to filing the notice of Default. This notice could be also referred to as an N.O.D. also known as Foreclosure Notice.

An N.O.D. is a notice sent to a homeowner that they have not paid their mortgage within the timeframes set by the lender. The Notice of Default is usually the very first document that is received from a homeowner who is behind in payments on a monthly basis. In California notice of default is the first legal document received by a homeowner. Notice of Default is the first document that is that is filed by a trustee and it is filed in the county in which the property is situated. This is the first step a lender must take during the foreclosure process.

The notice of Default dictates that if the amount due (plus additional legal costs) are not paid within the time frame specified the lender may decide to foreclose on the property of the borrower. Other parties who could suffer the consequences of foreclosure, such as the second mortgage holder, private note holder and an H.O.A. can also be provided with a copy of the notice. After it is recorded, the Notice of Default has been filed, the lender will need to wait for 90 days before proceeding to pursue foreclosure.

An N.T.S. also known as Notice of Trustee's sale is a form of notice of an auction open to the public. The N.T.S. is the next step of the California foreclosure process. it is the trigger for the sale date for the home. The notice of default is filed at least 90 days after the date of the initial Notification of Default.

The issuance of a Notice of Default is not a sign that a homeowner has lost control, but it does mean it's time to act. If you receive a Notice of Default is received , or the homeowner is concerned that one could be coming, an experienced short sale broker should be contacted to discuss the options and options available. There are a variety of options to stay out of foreclosure and short sales are one of them.

After it is clear that the Notice of Default has been filed, there are certain deadlines to meet. The fact that a lender is able to foreclose, it doesn't mean they'll foreclose, or that they are planning to foreclose.

If the NOD is not yet filed, consult an experienced professional to talk about your situation. The lender is not required to accept short sales, which is why the agent has to prepare the necessary information which tells the lender the full story of events in the event of the default.

The first requirement is an financial hardship or valid reason that is able to be proved and could affect the ability to to pay mortgages. This will have occurred between the time mortgage documents were signed and the present day. The possible difficulties include but aren't limited to the following:

Disability
Divorce/Separation
Ailment
Military Service
Lowered Income
Too Much Debt
Unemployment

Incarceration

Relocation of Jobs

Medical bills

Adjustment of ARM loan

Business Failure

Death of Spouse

Tenant loss

Second, there must be a month-long deficit in funds. The lender will ask for the financial worksheet be completed and signed to the home owner. The worksheet will list ALL household and personal expenses, including the current mortgage payment(s). Although it may seem difficult the process is actually quite simple as the lender utilizes the following formula:

monthly income minus total monthly expenditure equals negative cash flow

Thirdly, the homeowner has to be financially insolvent. Insolvency for a lender implies that there is no ability to pay the mortgage, and that there are more debts than assets or cash. If there are a few savings account for basic living expenses the lender is not obligated to exempt an applicant. However the lender will conduct a verification that the homeowner has assets that will enable them to pay their mortgage(s) in the present or in the near term.

While a short sale might appear daunting but the process is simple and efficient provided that a seasoned professional is chosen as the mediator of the deal.

If there isn't any kind of government incentive or loan that are offered that the homeowner is not able to be able to walk away with the proceeds of the deal.

The benefits of a quick sale include a more elegant exit, the elimination of ever having to mention the property was foreclosed upon in the future on mortgages or job applications, and the option to remain in the house during the time it is being transferred to a buyer.

The need for an agent who is not connected to the homeowner is essential since the lender will require an arms length agreement to be considered for Short sale loan approval.

The process itself is like the traditional sale. The homeowner might be still living in the home or might have already moved out. The main difference is that instead of stressing about fixing things or fixing things to make the most money the property is being sold "as-is" at an affordable market value.

The lender will decide the value of the property asking for a complete appraisal or an appraisal BPO (Broker Price Opinion). The report will give an updated value of the property on its date. After reviewing the report the lender could decide to release its lien for the amount of the loan as that is stated in the appraisal with or without 12percent.

Common seller expenses associated with normal sales are passed to the lender, to be paid out of their profits. This means that items such as settlement fees or fee for escrow, agent commissions and title insurance, tax bills that are not paid, HOA dues, etc. will be paid from the funds towards the loan. The lender will determine the an amount that they are willing to pay for each line item of the settlement statement. Therefore, it is not unusual for the commission of an agent to be cut or settlement fees to be reduced. The homeowner is not obliged to pay for anything.

In certain situations, where there is an excessive amount of in arrears HOA charges or a personal loans that are attached to the property the lender might not be willing to pay the cost. A seasoned short sale broker can to determine the best method to handle the situation, whether that is negotiations with the buyer to pay for them, or even negotiating the amount to a reasonable amount of payment.

Same inspections, and disclosure documents utilized to sell traditional properties are also available for short sales, too. The only difference between these two types is that the loanee must approve all conditions in the contract, and properties are sold"as-is" without seller-funded repairs, which includes termite damage.

Short selling a reverse mortgage

What happens to the property when there's reverse mortgage? The reverse mortgage can be described as a particular kind of mortgage for homeowners who are 62 or older. The idea behind them was to provide an additional income stream for seniors by taking advantage of the equity in their homes.

The homeowner surrenders the equity in their home and in return receives monthly installments as a source of income supplement. Contrary to traditional mortgages, which decrease in value as they pay off the reverse mortgage will increase in time as the interest accrues on the loan.

Similar to the traditional "forward" mortgages reverse mortgages can be secured with homeowners and turn into mortgages on the homes of their borrowers. In general, reverse mortgages become due and payable after borrowers are able to sell their homes or stop their occupation in them. Reverse mortgages also resemble forward mortgages because they are able to be short-sold for properties with them to be short-sold at a price less than their mortgage balances.

If the property is underwater which means that there is a reverse mortgage balance higher than market value the short sale may be beneficial for a homeowner. The same rules for an emergency would be applicable.

Similar to conventional mortgage loans, sometimes an option for a short sale can make more sense for a lender rather than closing on a home. If the option for the lender is to consider the cost and timeframes for foreclosure, or accepting 95% of the value of the property in a short sale, the short sale might be the best option to choose.

All reverse mortgage loans are not recourse loans which means that the borrower or estate of a borrower cannot be pursued for balances remaining.

A typical guideline for reverse mortgage short sales stipulate that homeowners who have reverse mortgages may short-sell their home to the lesser of mortgage balance or homes appraised value. The lender could also make out of the short sale's proceeds reasonable and normal costs- like a typical short sale. The costs could include , but aren't only limited to settlement costs as well as title insurance commissions for real estate transactions and so on.

If the person who financed the reverse mortgage has passed away in death, the lender could collaborate with an individual from the family or estate to buy the property through short sales. In contrast to a traditional sale the lienholder of the reverse mortgage is not required to enter into an arm's length deal. This could allow the house to remain in the family.

Chapter 7: Finding Your Hidden Gem

The ideal investment property that will make you money isn't right across the street waiting for you purchase it. Also, it won't magically show up in the news. To find the perfect real estate property that is suited to your requirements and generate regular income, you should be prepared to spend an hour or two researching. You'll need to play the role as a negotiator and investigator and draw out all the other abilities you might have thought you had.

Imagine this as finding a gem hidden. You've heard stories of the precious stone but you don't have any clues in the way to guide at the correct direction. Instead, you must be a tireless hunter looking.

The process of finding the ideal property is the same. There is a property out there However, whether it's given to your name or to someone else's is a matter that is entirely your decision and depends on the extent of your commitment.

Location

There's an old joke in the world of real estate (and even in many other industries) that states that the three key elements to be successful are "location, location and the location'. The most crucial aspect of buying real estate is to ensure that the property is located in the right location and is in been, or is likely to be in high demand.

Most of the time, the place will have a more impact on the profit as will the overall condition of the home. If you buy a house that is not in a good area is much more lucrative than purchasing a home in a poor area where no one buys.

In reality, many wealthy buyers are to find the perfect site to construct their dream home. And if they spot one of your homes located in a perfect location, they'll be happy to purchase the property from you in the hopes of demolishing the old home that is on the property.

The best method to purchase real estate is to imagine that you are purchasing the property for your own use. Do you reside in a place which is not kid-friendly and secured if you had children? Do you want to travel for miles before reaching the nearest supermarket? If you aren't able to find your family members living in a specific area and you are not sure if it will other people.

When you first explore an idea to invest in real estate with someone with previous experience in the business, you'll most probably be directed to select one that is in your local area due to the fact that it is close to your home and you have a good understanding of the area.

However, that's not always the best decision. While you might not desire to move, and you are in love with your neighborhood and all that's within it, it doesn't suggest that the place is financially prosperous. There are a variety of factors that determine if you should put your money in one particular area or not.

Even if you're familiar with the neighborhood and the locals, as well as the lifestyle of that area does not mean that you'll make money. This simply means that you'll be able to manage the area. If you do decide to make an investment close to home, should conduct your research in order to make sure you're certain that you will make the best decision possible.

The Increasing Population

Sometimes, finding an investment property is as easy as knowing where the inhabitants are. Population growth is one of the primary reasons you should consider the area you want to invest in.

It's just logical that areas that have the highest increase in population require more commercial and residential properties. Growing populations mean that more people will need a place to livein, which results in many jobs. The new job opportunities will in turn bring more people into the area.

In essence the end, areas with high population are the best option to buy a house. A high demand implies that you are able to negotiate a higher rent, and simultaneously, the chance of finding vacant properties are reduced.

Statistics indicate it is when an region increases by 3 people the area will require a new household. However, you shouldn't depend on this statistic due to the fact that not every house has the exact number of household members.

However, studying Metropolitan Statistical Area (MSA) data is extremely beneficial in gaining insight into population changes and the trends in housing. I strongly suggest that you conduct this prior to heading out to look around the area.

Supply and Demand

Each real property market adheres to the tried-and-true rule of supply and demand. Supply refers to the amount of properties on the market and demand is related to the number of individuals seeking properties to purchase or rent.

A perfect scenario for every real estate investor is an abundance of demand and low supply as this results in substantial rental income and fewer empty properties. It's not the case in the real world however it is possible, if you look at large cities and areas of high demand for property like New York and San Francisco. In the majority of areas, it's somewhere in the middle.

There are a few methods to assess the demand and supply of real estate in an location. These variables will help you decide if purchasing a house in that area would be a good investment for your portfolio.

Building Permits

The most trustworthy methods to assess the degree of demand and supply is to look at the report on building permits. The building permit the government-issued authorization for any kind of construction work, regardless of whether it is for a brand new or an existing construction. Building permit information can give you an accurate picture of what's happening in a specific market. If the amount of building permits is growing it means that the demand will the need.

Absorption Rate

The absorption rate refers to the rate that people purchase or lease newly constructed properties. A market worth investing in must have a high rate of absorption, meaning that demand is high and the buildings were quickly rented or sold typically within a matter of months.

Absorption rates that are high indicate that properties are being'swallowed immediately. For example, if there are 500 houses that are on the market in the area A high absorption rate indicates that in few months, the inventory has run out.

If an area is "overflowing" with homes that have been on the market for a longer amount in time market generally, it is an indication that the demand isn't as high than the available inventory, as well as is a indication that you need to look elsewhere to find potential investment opportunities.

In contrast to building permit reports that are readily accessible, absorption figures aren't accessible to all. Remember when I said you must have an effective team to be successful? This is where appraisers as well as real estate professionals can be of assistance. Most of them have been Certified Commercial Investment Member and in the majority of cases, they'll be able to find out more about the rates of absorption.

Rate of Vacancy

The rate of vacancy, which is the proportion of units that are available in the region you're considering purchasing, is incredibly crucial. If you know the rate of vacancy it is easier to estimate how your property going to be performing. In the end, you don't be investing in an area where homes are known to remain empty for a long time due to the lack of demand.

Monitor Local Auctions

If demand is high the chances are that there will be more auctions for properties. Take a look at one or more auctions in the region you're considering investing in to find out whether the properties are actually selling and how many are fighting for bids on it. If there's a significant amount of bidding going on, it could indicate of whether the market is in good shape.

The length of availability

Another aspect that could provide a clue to the market and demand for an region is the duration of the properties that are available you're considering. Check when the property became available , and then for the length of time they remain for on the market. If the property has been in the market for too long or take a long time in order to rent them out or removed, then it's probable that the demand is not high.

The Progress

It is possible to be deceived by the appearance. Sometimes, even if it appears that a location is going to bring in lots of cash immediately, it may not be exactly the same over the long run. Some areas are the same for years.

For instance, an area could look nice in the present due to the strip mall just a mile further. However, what happens if the managers of the strip mall do not take care to keep it in good condition and eventually, customers choose to move the business to another location? Always be on the lookout for signs of growth in the region you're considering investing in. Two major indicators that will tell you if the region is expanding or not:

"Stalk" the Retailers

Retailers, particularly large national chains, do not start up in specific regions based on what they feel. There are countless millions of dollars in stake every time they launch an additional location and therefore must be certain that the location is worth investing in. This is why these big chains are backed by an expert group who have invested a considerable amount of time debating the advantages and disadvantages of opening in this area.

The fact that there's the possibility of opening (or just recently launched) the store indicates that the location is expanding. This could be an indication that it's appropriate to open a store as well.

It's similar to watching the top investors such as Warren Buffet do and which businesses they invest their money into. You'll still have to conduct your own research but at the very least, you're now aware that you're heading in the right direction.

Follow the Roads

Another sign that an area is expanding and advancing is the building of new highways and roads. A quiet hillside town with a gorgeous river view may be peaceful in the past, as it was accessible only by the treacherous, long road. However, if the government of the state decides to construct tunnels that will make getting more efficient and safer and safer, it's likely there will be many more people who want to move to the area.

It doesn't have to be a brand new road or bridge. Sometimes, it's an area of a major city that had public transportation at one time unaccessible. If there are a few bus stops are constructed or the construction of a new rail station is constructed in the vicinity, it is likely the area will see a surge of new business activity in the neighborhood.

In short, any transportation-related development can be a sign that an area is improving (or will about to improve). But, make sure to verify if the projects be completed since it's not unusual to find roads that remain under construction for a number of years.

Distinction from Major Hubs

Your distance from your home and essential amenities like supermarkets, gas stations parks and transportation hubs shouldn't be too long.

If you don't have children, you might not be concerned about the necessity to have schools within the vicinity however the tenants or buyers could be. Check the area to see whether there are schools within a short distance. This can only increase the number of potential buyers and tenants larger, meaning that your odds of making money are greater.

Also, it is recommended to verify how far you are from the location you're interested in and the nearest major city. Many people who can't afford to live near to their job might consider moving to suburbs, where the rent and property costs are lower. But if the property is far from where you work, you might not be able to give up the significantly longer commute time for a cheaper rent.

Natural Nature-related

Certain areas are more susceptible to natural disasters like earthquakes, tornadoes or floods. For example, if there's an area with a river and there's a massive flood every now and then throughout the year, it may cause a fear in prospective buyers, but it could may also make the region generally less likely to grow into an important economic hub.

While this might not be an issue in the event that you intend to lease the property (since you'll pay for all the costs and costs of renovations and repairs) however, it will be if you attempt to sell the property. No one wants to purchase an investment property that they know they'll have to invest many hours and money to fix each year because of natural catastrophes.

Crime Rates

Everyone doesn't want to reside in a neighborhood with a high crime rate. While it's not possible to find an area that is 100 100% safe but a neighbourhood's potential for criminal activity is a major factor for most buyers , especially those with children.

If you are looking for a home make sure to contact the local law enforcement and government officials to inquire about crime statistics. The police in your area can assist you in determining whether there are any indicted sex offenders in the desired area. It is also possible to contact the local newspaper, who will probably have plenty of stories and information to give to you.

Chapter 8: Recreation Real Estate Properties

In the two previous chapters, we have looked at residential and commercial properties. Now we'll look at the third kind of property, which is known by the name of recreational property. In this chapter, I'll explain the significance of these kinds of properties as well as advantages and disadvantages of investing in these kinds of properties.

What exactly is Recreational Real Estate?

The word"recreation" is often synonymous with joy and pleasure and with good reason. These properties are intended to provide relaxation and rest to whomever you let it out to. The majority of these properties are thought to include ranches, farms and waterfronts, zoos and wild life reserves etc. People love beautiful locations for retirement and unwinding, and more often than not nature is the ideal backdrop to escape from the bustle in the modern world.

I'm sure that you've seen TV shows that show distinctive homes built by people for recreation purposes. These are homes for recreation which are designed to give the owner leisure and enjoyment. There are many unique designs across the globe and are designed to be used as second homes. However, you may also decide to use it as your primary residence.

If you intend to lease out the property as a recreation estate, you'll have to decide if you would like to let it open to the public or reserve it for private tenants. For example, if you purchase a tiny cabin near the forest, or a beachfront shack that you can let it to families to enjoy a vacation on a seasonally-based basis. If you have an area of land that you wish to transform into a leisure space that is accessible to people, you can look into making it an animal park or wildlife reserve and similar.

When you're dealing with huge areas of land that you would like to lease to rent, you'll be required to adhere to a set of regulations set by the authorities in the first. You'll need to have your land zoned -

this is the process through the relevant authorities of the government decide on how the land will be utilized. It is possible that you won't be able to purchase an enormous piece of land , as is needed from the home you wish to lease; typically the municipal authorities in your area are able to zone large areas of land according to the seasons. It is necessary be able to follow a variety of legal procedures before you can get permission to use the land. Talk to a lawyer and let them assist you with the steps to ensure you get the most of it!

After you've got the land under your control and are able to begin building an animal sanctuary, a reserve or cabin regardless of what your requirements are - you'll need to consider the typical features expected with any real property. Like the homes as well as commercial properties there is a need to install standard fixtures, among them -

Fences and gates that mark what is the boundary of your property This is especially crucial in big, public spaces like parks or zoos, as there are animals that must be cared for and also a noisy public to be controlled.

Cabins and sheds that have water and electricity If you're offering an escape in the woods or a spot to camp, they will be sought-after as your tenants will want to be comfortably

Waste disposal systemsare essential, since you aren't able to afford to let your property be a dump.

Transport facilities will assist travelers travel to or out of rural areas. It is essential to organize for your guests to move about, especially when the retreat is far from retail stores as well as other amenities. If you don't provide the facilities they require, it may become a little uncomfortable for them. You must try to keep cabs that have drivers who can drive passengers around.

You could also provide the essentials in order for your guests to purchase them in the event of an emergency.

As with commercial and residential properties, there's no definitive rule of thumb for the fixtures sought-after. The fixtures will need be designed to meet the function that the house is being used for. For example, if it is a zoo you're opening then it is mandatory to have fencing around individual cages to safeguard the animals and the visitors. The installation of electricity in this case could be a waste of cash. However when you rent out an outdoor cabin and the tenants are likely to require at a minimum basic of amenities such as a few lights to look out for regardless of whether they are seeking a rural experience. Be aware of these factors when you make a decision to purchase recreational real estate.

Pros

Since the majority of recreation properties are near to nature in one way or other You are guaranteed of being able to rent your property. Zoos and reserves are likely to have all-year-round guests, however residences and cabins could have a more seasonal the natural world. However, you'll make a significant amount of cash, particularly during the summer months. A growing number of people are embracing nature and seeking rental cabins for the season and get a true experience in nature and you won't be left with a shortage of tenants to rent your property to. It is important to do some research and study regions that are well-known for their tourist places. It is best to pick places that are well-known throughout the year, not just during specific months.

In this case, you'll be able to easily have investors from other companies invest with you. They'll be impressed by your selection of investment, and will decide to partner with you in order to make a profit. You could join forces with someone who is interested in investments in recreational properties. You can also increase the size of your property by utilizing their assistance. You will be able to make a lot from your recreational property investment if you pick the right type.

If you can offer a number of extra services and amenities like fishing, hiking, rafting and more, you'll attract an enormous number of visitors interested in participating in these activities. It is possible to form partnership with a few locals who will manage your property on your behalf. they can turn into a successful business venture offering more than just accommodation for customers. It is important to pick the ideal area and the most suitable people to partner with. In one way or another it is likely that you will meet one or another who is looking to lease out your home.

Conservationists and animal lovers are among the tenants that will be flocking towards your premises. In contrast to the common people who arrive, stay some time, unwind and then go home the property, these tenants are focused on the specific services you can provide. This means you'll have clients to lease out even in the season when it is not in use, and you can use their knowledge in the field of natural sciences to enhance the services you provide! For instance, if renting your cabin to marine scientists you can ask the person to host some exhibitions for tourists at just a few dollars!

An ideal option is to purchase a property which is still in its an early stage of development. Prices for these areas are lower, and you'll be in a position to spend more to renovate it and set it up in the way you prefer. If the land behind is allowed to be developed will be developed, you'll definitely be able to generate good money from your home!

Cons

If you do manage to find tenants, you'll make quite a bit of cash. However, the majority of property for recreational use will be seasonal. This means that in the off-season, you will be feeling unsatisfied, with a small amount of cash relative to tourist seasons. Additionally, be aware of the intended group-not all are familiar with the wilderness. The majority of them are urban dwellers and, therefore getting away to a lodge in the woods might not be a pleasurable holiday, especially for the youngsters of the present. You must make sure you package your offer well and include additional services to lure them into hiring from your.

Maintaining the property could be a challenge. Being in the wilderness means there are numerous daily chores that must be done to ensure that the property is in good and living conditions. The chores could include everything from cutting wood for fires to shoveling snow. If you are able to afford spending all day doing these things throughout the period that there are no tenants you might have to employ the locals to help. It can be quite expensive and labor-intensive.

Tenants may also be complaining that there aren't adequate drainage and water systems and heating systems, for instance. The true city-bred children are also expected to arrive with amenities like Wi-Fi and internet and phone signal, that they might or might not get in remote locations. It is important to be patient when dealing with these tenants who are grumpy and organize for anything they need urgently.

Given that you are building a property that is near nature and nature there is a likely chance that you'll be subject to severe weather patterns. Prepare for thunder storms, snowstorms, landslides, heat waves, and any other natural catastrophe. Prepare contingency plans in case of emergency, and ensure that you have at minimum two medical facilities accessible to your tenants to ensure that they do not get in a panic.

You must be aware of the risks animals can pose to your property as well as your tenants. The properties close to woods, in particular, will need to be secured to keep wild animals from gaining entry however you won't be able to take any action regarding raccoons and rats as well as the small creatures that might sneak in regardless. Give your tenants the appropriate level of security to ensure they are safe and can enjoy the outdoors to the maximum. If there have been instances of humans being attacked by wild animals, it is essential to act immediately to prevent incident like this from happening in the future.

As we mentioned earlier, recreation areas are subject to the desires and desires of a variety of concerned authorities. Renovation or expansion is a major challenge for the homeowner. If you own commercial or residential properties, you are free to grow as much as you want to and the legal procedure should take only few days or weeks to process. If you are on recreational land, however it is possible that you will be waiting months for permits to be granted and you'll need to inform the authorities of every step you take, as the safety of the people could be in danger if you don't.

Locating locals to stay at your disposal can be difficult. Many times they are located in communities that are tightly knit and have a difficult time accept outsiders. However, if you can spin the situation to your advantage and provide them with jobs that are generous to gain their trust, which will make a huge difference in ensuring that your property is secure and secure.

It is evident that out of the three kinds of real estate that you can invest in, the recreational type will be the type that requires the longest. If you are a novice to buying real estate for investment, you might prefer to avoid this type of investment because it takes an enormous amount of time, money and effort which you may or might not have at your available. However If you've been in the business for a while and are familiar with the basics and have money to spare, then recreational real estate can be a profitable investment that can bring lots of money for you! Engage the locals to turn it into a reputable tourist attraction, and you'll discover that you can to make a substantial lump sum of money, compared to commercial or residential properties!

Container homes

Container homes are a new type of investment. They are modern-day investment options and aren't like the previous kinds of investments. In this article we will examine containers in depth and explore their distinct aspects in depth.

Meaning

The name implies that "container houses" are constructed from "containers". You may be wondering what the purpose of the containers actually are. They are basically containers used for shipping. These are cargo containers that are utilized to transport cargo from one place to another.

They are huge in size and accommodate thousands of kilograms of cargo. They are extremely robust and resistant to damage and wear.

These containers are fantastic storage options and are also used for go-downs by a variety of both large and small companies.

If you are looking for a simple home to build can consider them as housing alternatives. They are very durable and can be used to construct entire homes using them. They are readily available and you can purchase them from a container business.

They aren't conventional, but these kinds of homes are slowly becoming popular. There is no need for a large purchase and are able to stay within a set budget. When you use these, you'll be amazed at how gorgeous they are. You can use them as a second option and not as a permanent option. You'll be able to enjoy the benefits of having a second residence that you can lease out or own.

How do I

In the case of containers for homes there are some basic steps you have to take. Let's examine these steps in greater detail: The first step is looking for the most suitable location you could set up an apartment in your container. Container houses can be built at any place provided that it is simple to move the container. Find a site that you like. The majority of people prefer areas which are completely covered with grass since they are great container home locations. There are many offers on properties. It's also a good idea to search for an area for recreation with something natural like the mountains or waterfalls. This can increase the value of your land and make your house far more desirable.

Next step planning the design of your container home. Find some ideas and pick a container size that fits your property the most. You can have only one container or layer up by putting one on top of another. It is possible to create an aduplex if you wish.

Next step looking for a container seller that can deliver the container. The majority of these suppliers are situated near the coast, and you should look for the most reliable one. Check out their website and determine if you like their designs. Certain companies offer specific designs that are tailored to your preferences. They can be provided with an idea of design and ask them to design a custom packaging for you.

It is the next thing to do, drive to the nearest store and purchase the container. It is possible that you will need to travel quite a amount if you are located far from the coastline. It is also necessary to have an appropriate vehicle that will aid in the transport of containers back on your property.

After you have purchased the containeror containers, you need to take them to the location you want to use them. Following that, you need to put them in the correct spot. Like we said before that you should think about your house's layout prior to placing the containers in the right locations. It is possible to create an apartment duplex from it.

After everything is set Once everything is in place, you can decorate themhowever you'd prefer. You can paint them from the inside and decorate the outside with a style you are comfortable with.

You can then lease it out, or relocate yourself.

Pros

There are numerous advantages to purchasing container homes. One of the advantages is that you are able to easily build an apartment in a container. It is not necessary to make up a complex strategy and it shouldn't take longer than a week to select a container house for your family. It is also not necessary to wait for a long time before you can have your house prepared. It's as simple as searching for the perfect spot to build your house and the appropriate container that can be transformed into your own home.

Another advantage is lower costs. In addition to the cost of land it is also true that the containers won't cost you a lot. Therefore, you will save a significant amount of dollars by buying containers for your home.

The affordable cost makes it a great second residence. You can increase your real estate portfolio by investing in container houses.

The unique design of these homes lets you become as creative as you can. It can be decorated in any way you would like.

It is possible to easily transport your container homes well. The container can be emptied of its contents, then connect it to a truck that will allow you to change the site of your house and move it to a beautiful region. It's similar to having a mobile home.

Cons

The primary drawback of this kind of investment is the fact that it can be difficult to move the container from one location to another. It will be a challenge to transport the containers , and it is the possibility of damage you have to keep in mind.

Because containers are made out of metal, the chance of rusting is quite high. The house in your container may get rusty and you'll need to pay for the removal of the rust off of the container. It is more dangerous to stack the containers on top of one another since they may burden the container on top.

It can be quite challenging to adapt to a container house. It's a huge change from a normal home, and you'll need to make a variety of adjustments. It can be a challenge to incorporate furniture into the container houses.

They are the various advantages and disadvantages of homes in containers. Overall, they're the best investment choice for you.

Chapter 9: Rental Property Tips

The rental property may appear to be the most secure option from afar. There are dangers, especially when you consider the various elements that could make your rental property empty. To help you understand the potential risks associated with rental properties and ways to mitigate these risks, here is an overview of the most crucial elements.

Pets

Are you able to allow animals? A lot of large apartment complexes run by REITs, real estate investment companies and REITs are not able to accommodate pets. They don't want to let go of the profits the cleaning of the apartment after pets have been in. Also, there is a greater possibility that several units could be vacant simultaneously.

If apartments allow pets, the charges can be staggering. The renter could have to pay as much as $400 to deposit a pet per pet. The pet owner may also be charged for the cost of pet rent per month that could range between $10-$100 per month per pet. One must have a passion for their pets in order to pay for a premium. There is also the matter about how many pets a pet is allowed to have. The usual limit is two. There are sizes and breed restrictions in some apartments. After a person has moved out of the apartment, if it requires a more thorough cleaning due to the pet's smell or caused damage to the walls or doors, they will forfeit their entire deposit. This is the reason why some apartment complexes weigh the possibility of having pets versus the cost they incur and have decided to not allow pets.

For those who own one property and is trying to rent itout, there are other considerations that need to be taken into consideration.

If your pet causes damage to the carpet, you require it to be cleaned or to tear it out to replace the carpet.

If you notice damage to door trim, door window trim, tile or any other flooring because of your pet, you need to repair it.

The majority of people rent an apartment in a community that may not be a happy place in the event that a noisy animal creates noise during the night and daytime.

There is a chance that you will lose more than 50% of potential tenants who are searching for an apartment.

The fourth option must be the deciding factor. If the property sits empty for the entire year, do you have the capacity to pay the loan? Are you paying an excessive amount of costs to maintain the property? Naturally, when you don't get paid rent, you are liable for expenses. In cold areas it is essential to maintain the heat so pipes don't freeze. In hot climates it is imperative to keep the air conditioner running or else you risk causing getting mold. The cost of running the air conditioner for keeping the area livable will take money from your pocket.

Do you have the money to let your property sit empty? For the majority of landlords, it's not possible. There are some circumstances where money is the most when deciding whether for allowing pets. The decision is based on the space you own the rental property. It all boils down to the location.

A town in the college is a location that is populated by renters. The renters might or might not own pets, and the majority will not be because they're studying. If you live in an area that has many renters, but not enough rentals and you are not in a position to rent, then you don't have to let pets. In areas where homes are in short supply or you're in competition with apartment complexes that are large it is possible to be flexible about your pet policy.

You should have a Pet Policy

If you decide to permit pets, make sure you establish a strict policy for pets which is followed. For instance, if you permit dogs and cats it is important to specify how many pets can reside in the house as well as any breeds you are not allowed to allow or the weight limitations. The more precise your pet policy is, the easier to draw the attention of renters should it be violated.

It is also possible to request the amount to cover the cost of cleaning up after your pets.

The Deposit

Always get a deposit. It is legal to request the one and the last month's rent along with a security deposit. It is contingent on the amount of rent and the location you're looking to rent. It is possible that the "last" months rent could be considered also a deposit, but make sure you know what can't happen when someone leaves, with regard in the amount of deposit.

Deposit money will be used to pay to make repairs based on the damages caused by the tenant. It is generally called something that isn't "reasonable." It's true carpets do become filthy. Paint can be slightly smudged caused by moving furniture inside or out of the home. Damage caused by a tenant who hit their fist into the wall, or their dog was pawing at the door, or a person spray painted the walls are not considered to be unreasonable damage. Deposits are intended to compensate for the problems that aren't reasonable, or could be intentional damage.

Also, you should be sure that you're not being slapped with a hefty bill for rent. There have been instances where people go out in the night because they can't pay their rent, but still insist on the refund of their deposit as well as last month's rent they paid. It is essential to have at least two months' worth of rent to ensure your security in case you have an unpaid rental or a missed payment or if someone leaves without warning.

While the emphasis has been on deposits and pets throughout this article, you'll have gained an understanding of the principal theme of renting property. The danger is that you'll have to pay for repairs or not paying rent, so the most effective way to protect yourself against this possibility is to sign a secure tenancy agreement for your renters. The renter must sign an agreement which legally binding. It will detail the amount of deposit, when rent will be due when rent is due and what happens if they fail to pay rent for several months. This will ensure that you recover some of your losses , or at least keep the deposit that you've earned since the beginning of the contract.

Do not let a tenancy contract expire, and get permission if there's going to be a transition from the yearly lease to a month-to- month lease, and with all necessary requests as to when the deadline for the written notice of any end agreement should be sent.

Chapter 10: Reits And Real Estate Investment Tips

REITs as well as real estate investment organizations are distinct, and each will offer their own advice. They're merged here since the advice is short.

REITs

90percent of tax-deductible income of REITs has to be returned to owners in the form dividends.

The investment you make in REITs is liquid, unlike other real estate transactions.

You can buy and sell REIT shares much as you would do shares on exchanges.

There are minimal investment requirements REITs have, which are different from other investment properties.

It is important to evaluate the growth in earnings that is a result of increased occupancy and rising rents in addition to assessing the cost savings and new opportunities for business.

Study the management team as it is the management team that will determine if a property is renovated, or if additional services are provided and assist in increasing the demand for the property.

You must be aware of wage growth. It directly impacts the rate at which rent increases. Rent increases could reduce the number of renters, and even cause renters to be unable to remain in the house they've rented for many years. There's a line of difference between increasing rent in order to earn more money and making sure that the property is rent-free. The management team needs to be aware of the best options for rent market to ensure that they are not denying the possibility of earning income in the hopes of earning more.

Real Estate Investment Groups

The primary distinction between the REIT and a real estate investment groups, is that the former is a real estate investment group, while the REIT is actually a trust you are able to join. Both be invested in rentals as well as land. Real estate investment firms tend to invest in commercial and apartment structures, and not vacant land that they can build upon in the future. The property is also yours rather than a corporation that is the owner as well as selling share shares.

Check the area that the property is situated in.

Are the local economies suffering or is it able to support the rental rates to the properties?

Are the team members of the management effective?

Consider the earning potential.

Also, you should consider the rising rental rates, occupancy, new opportunities for business, and the potential services that could be provided.

Similar to REITs, REITs must have a large occupancy in order to generate profits. In addition, a rent increase in a region which isn't able to support such an increase could lead to empty spaces. It all comes down to the property management team succeeds in keeping an existing situation in which you make money, but without having to take greater than what the market is able to support.

Chapter 11: Homeowners Gain Smart

What, if anything, did this shift? Homeowners started having an internet connection. They got more informed. They were taught to look around. They were instructed to talk with at least three agents and had prepared questions for every interview. The realtors were suddenly required to compete, and a lot of us were used to it.

Homeowners have stopped calling office numbers from those yellow pages. Instead they did their research and researched local realtors, gathered numerous market analysis, and conducted interviews before taking a shrewd decision to market their home.

And to make things even more difficult even more, as the market was at its peak every single person, including their brother decided to obtain an authorization. Perhaps those of us who were working in the industry could have made it appear so simple and so more people jumped onto the bandwagon. It was like everyone was aware of the term "real estate agent. This meant you could not be sure that your area of influence to provide you with constant leads.

The prices of homes were on the sky and buyers were purchasing. Lending institutions were offering loans with no docs, and the buyers didn't have to prove their income. The decision to approve them was based on the income they claimed to earn. Banks didn't consider whether the buyer were able to pay off their mortgages but they desired to see the loan paid off so they could offer it to another mortgage broker to make an income.

It was a turbulent period, and one of the causes for the economic downturn that we're experiencing today. In the end, the whole process of selling a home was easy. If you were fortunate enough to find a property that was available, you were almost assured of a quick closing as well as the leads you'd receive from the numerous call-to-actions that aren't as often these days.

Today, it's much harder to secure an entry at all or even getting it to the final table. It requires a lot of work, and the market is crowded. The demand for home owners is higher nowadays as do buyers as well.

Beware of Buyers!

What does all of this mean for me? This meant the ads weren't coming to me! I needed to locate these listings... as well, and honestly... I did not know how to go about it. So I did the most reasonable thing I could do. I sought out buyers as they appeared to be easier to find.

I hosted open houses for realtors that actually had listings. I spent a lot of money advertising in coupons magazines. I irritated my family and friends, neighbors and friends with numerous reminder emails (Hey do not forget me should you know someone in need of selling or buying!) I also created and distributed regular newsletters (most of them probably ended up right into the garbage) as well as friendly messages when I'd run across my friends at the store. Don't forget to include the Welcome Spring postcards, the "I'm so grateful for all my customers & Friends" cards around Thanksgiving and those Happy Holidays postcards. I was a thorn in the side when I look back on the incident. Yikes!

What happened to all the effort and money? The answer is that I found some qualified buyers. A majority of the time however, I was in the streets showing houses for 10-12 hours each day to prospective buyers who were unqualified or simply window shopping because I did not take the time to understand how to properly qualify them. The phone would be ringing on a Sunday evening at 5pm, with buyers telling me they must see the house they were interested in that evening. Therefore, I would put on a coat and head across the street to greet them during the freezing cold. 99.9 percent times, people have never got the home they needed to visit right away. Even more so I'd have to spend months with buyers and then have them contact me on

Monday to say that they had have ended up purchasing the house as a FSBO! Are you able to relate?

Unfortunately, buyers took the life off of me. I was exhausted from searching for warm leads. I was annoyed by buyers who were unjust. To be honest in retrospect, I can solely blame myself. I wasn't sure how to select and select the most suitable clients to work. I was in desperate need of help, so I spent my time with all of them. I was unaware that I had any control over how I ran my own business.

My company suffered. I considered collaborating with someone who was their buyer's representative so that I could ride the coattails of someone else for a few months. I was thinking it would be more beneficial for someone to be give to me lead leads for returning to them a large portion of my commission.

However, something got me off my feet. I thought about the top performers at my workplace. Why didn't they run through the buyers? What was the reason they were operating "normal" office hours? I did not visit the office, even though I was printing listing for buyer shows at 6 pm on a Saturday night. They had inventories, and huge inventories. What was their method of doing it? I was on the hunt to figure out the answer.

Chapter 12: Real Estate Holding

Twenty-five years ago, when I had an apartment building portfolio I was learning about multi-family management through"trial and terror. "trial and terrified" method. With so many properties and tenants, as well as so much going wrong every single day, I was never able to keep up let alone getting ahead. I made every error in the book, and possibly made a few others up. It was more about managing by crisis than management based on objective. The four-year real estate management experience has taught me a lot. But the most important lesson I learned from it was "there must be an easier method."

There's a better method. After my apartment building were sold, I listened to John Schaub lecture. He said, "You don't manage real estate; you manage people." The light was on. (Where was the man in the time I was desperate for him?) John explained various ways to convince and encourage tenants to be more responsible and not be disruptive to landlords. At that point, he was getting my full attention. It became apparent my perspective that, if could cut down on the amount of management I had to do and have more properties to manage and plenty of time to pursue other interests. The tips and suggestions I've included are based on my personal experience as well as the experiences of other people who were willing to share their knowledge with me.

The property you wish to let. I will be short and direct. The more well-maintained the house (inside the property and outside) is, the more desirable the tenant will be and less problems that may arise later on. If the property needs to be improved take it care of it now before even considering finding an applicant. If you've done your research at the process of acquisition you are aware of what has to be fixed and what the cost will be, the time it takes to finish it and who's going to complete it. That's enough for now.

Finding the prospective tenant. Ads in the local classifieds will work when you write about the your property, its address as well as the amount of rent, a contact number that is not your personal home phone, and include the statement, "Be sure to ask about our Discount Rent Program." This will result in numerous calls and inquiries from interested parties. (More regarding this Discount Rent Program in a minute). Additionally, I've used flyers about the rental distributed out to the neighborhood. Neighborhood residents tend to refer those they'd like to be neighbors with.

Then, in North Carolina, I found two great sources for tenants. One was the many employers located in the Research Triangle Park. Each firm had their individual relocation departments. They were extremely helpful in assisting tenants who were moving into the area and also giving notices to employees regarding available housing. Another source was an association consisting of property investors that regularly met to discuss possibilities and issues with one another.

We soon began sharing leads from tenants.

Signs are effective. I have put numbers for bedrooms as well as bathrooms on the lower part on the sign. Anyone who has called"For Rent "For Rent" sign has looked around the exterior of the house, the neighborhood and may have talked to some neighbors. They are satisfied with what they've seen so far, and are in the process of making the decision. They'd like to see the inside.

I inform them that it is not the policy of the company to show houses. They must visit the office to retrieve the key, deposit an $35.00 security deposit on the key, then view the house on their own, and return the key back to the office to receive a return of their deposit. (A copy of their driver's license is required.) I've seen people travel for up to an hour to return and pick up the keys. This is only one more stage in the process of obtaining a key.

In a note, it is dangerous to make use of this deposit system if your home is currently in the process of being rented.

ASSERTING THE PROSPECTIVE Tenant. Now, your goal is to find the "IDEAL Tenant."

A good tenant would be a family that sees the home as their "home" not as a "house" which they "rent." They'll have the ability to pay for all the monthly expenses associated of "home owning." Their financial responsibility is worried about their credit score as well as their image within the community. A perfect family is one that enjoys the "pride that they own" regardless of their circumstances aren't ripe for ownership in the present moment.

By including the rental amount and security amount in your advertisement for rent you've taken the first step in identifying the potential tenant. They are aware of what it will cost each month.

The location and the type of single-family home you're offering is the vital element of the qualification process. I've spoken to thousands of S/F investor over the last 20 years about their achievements and failures when it comes to managing rental properties. John Schaub's description of an ideal rental home is to be the most accurate so far. He wrote, "A 3/2 with a garage with two cars (attached) but without a pool, situated in an area of middle class where the houses are neat and tidy and my house is the only one on the block is what I've come across as ideal." Looking back at my own experiences and tribulations with S/Fs I think he's correct.

If your home is in a poor condition and is located situated in an area that is difficult it will be a magnet for hard-working and shabby prospective tenants. (I prefer to own a rental home in John's neighborhood rather than four cheap houses in a bad location that have numerous issues.) In the reverse, it is. The more appealing the first impression your property gives, the more quality tenants you'll be able to draw.

The most effective way to test any person for anything is to have an individual meeting with all parties involved. Your expertise in counseling can be extremely beneficial. I don't ever tell potential clients (or anyone else in fact) that I'm the owner of the property. I'm just a manager who was hired to run the property. Following, as part of the qualifying process, you will need to fill out the RENTAL APPLICATION. It requires all fundamental information about the applicant, as well as other applicants who plan to reside in your home--the more details, the more accurate. The form I use has a distinct space for the tenant to sign to sign the credit report. Make the form yourself (a excellent place to find the majority of the information you'll require is a bank application). After many questions and responses on both sides, you'll get a better idea of whether the applicants match what you're seeking. Inform the applicants that you will reach them by phone when you've confirmed the details they provided and also after you've met with other applicants for the lease. If you are happy with your findings, and you are comfortable with your impressions of the applicants, set up an additional meeting to go over the details and confirm the lease.

THE LEASE: Remember, you manage people, not real estate. The lease you sign and the degree to which the tenants comprehend it prior to signing will decide how many problems you'll face. The goal of every lease is to establish who is accountable for what and at what time. Do not be scared of long leases. Seven pages single-spaced isn't unusual. There are five key points that the lease must address every contingency and responsibility in a clear manner; it must be legally valid; you should review the entire document word-for-word together with all the people who will be signing the document. You should never alter one clause in the lease, or make any changes in any way (give an inch , and you'll be able to increase the amount) Also, you should not permit anyone to use the "unsigned" lease from your office.

The laws regarding landlord-tenant relations vary between states counties to counties and the city from city it is essential to seek legal advice from a professional. It is advisable to have your CPA go over it as well. This is not the purpose of this document to go over in depth the workings for some most effective leasing strategies however, let me go over some of the best aspects.

Motivated people are motivated by incentives and rewards and not with punishment. When I offer discounted rent to payment received before 1pm on the day that the rent is due I've found that the majority of people are content to make payments on time or even early.

The reason I have a "self-insurance" program serves as an incentive to keep appliances and equipment running. I will reduce rent in exchange for any repairs up to a specific dollar amount. Tenants are more likely to take control of their property since it's their duty to do so.

In addition at the time of my move to North Carolina, I started my pay-by-credit card plan. In the lease contract , there is a specific clause that states that they have authorised me in advance to access their credit account (all required details are added in the lease) to pay rent fully if they call the office and inform me to make the payment. The lease also permits me to charge rent to their credit card accounts should the rent not be paid within five days from when the date of due. When the tenant I managed to get who left unannounced and a bit behind on his rent payments. The credit-card-payment-plan was very helpful in bringing him current.

I have a Christmas program and several members have signed up throughout the years. The gross annual rent, then divide it into ELEVEN months, instead of 12. This will give the tenant the 12th month of rent for free that is December, in the event the lease is signed at the 1st of January. This is perfect for planning a vacation for the tenant as well.

In second place to running water, pets can ruin a home faster than any other thing. I prefer no pets. However, If "Fifi" is truly an important person in the household, well is it my intention to end any work relationship. Pet deposits are greater than the deposit for rent. The monthly cost to "Fifi" is 20% rent increase. Sorry , there are no exclusions to this policy: "See, it says that in the lease agreement that you sign." The tenants decide to look for another landlord, accept to pay the pet rent, or decide that "Fifi" is more content with their family at home.

The lease should advise the tenants purchase their own tenants-contents insurance policy and warn them of the consequences if they fail to obtain one. As a landlord, you should discuss with your experienced insurance agent regarding umbrella insurance policies for risk. An umbrella policy of five million dollars insurance policy is not expensive and lets you sleep soundly at the end of the night.

The other clause I have in my lease reads "Good neighbors policy." The clause was added by me some time back to make sure that tenants are aware that they are immediately evicted when their behavior and the behavior of their "pets," their actions or the actions of their guests disturbs the neighborhood. The clause should be as robust as law allows. It is a good way to ensure that things are kept silent. The use of fireworks, firearms or explosives of any kind are not permitted under any circumstances.

One final point before we proceed. There are some truly horrific reports of chemical storage that was improperly handled which have leaked onto ground, and then soaked in the groundwater table. I have added a lengthy paragraph that outlines the tenant's responsibilities and obligations in relation to their storage and leakage and disposal of EPA approved substance. At no time will there ever be any of these information or statements regarding the property for any reason whatsoever. The EPA is a firm believer in taking action against the owner of record, regardless of who and when or how pollution caused damage occurred. So be cautious before you purchase real estate, if you lease the property to tenants or should someone give you a deed in place of foreclosure on a note that he has to pay you. If you haven't assessed the physical property, place everything on hold.

until you're able to get it checked by experts on the spot.

Other documents that are required A few other tools to keep things in order between your landlord and you.

Key deposit receipts - is refunded at the expiration of lease after return the keys. Make sure you change the locks at the when a tenant leaves.

Inspection agreement The tenant and the tenant have conducted the "walk-through" to the building to ensure that everything is in order, functioning and in good working order. The walk-through will take place after the expiration of the lease, before deposits are reimbursed.

A listing of emergency phone numbers: Fire police, Fire and so on. However, I have included an emergency number where I can be reachable. My office hours are 9-5 every day from 9 to 5.

REGISTRY KEEPING in a nutshell my system for keeping records is the KISS formula: keep it simple (accurate and up-to-date)

It's a joke. I've always advised tenants on the lease to send their rent payments each month three days in advance to a particular account at the bank that is specified. The tenant knows that the rent paid with the deposit slip that is filled out must be sent by mail and not delivered by hand for the system to function effectively. When the lease is signed, I hand the tenant twelve deposit slips as well as twelve envelopes prepaid for self-addressing that are provided to the tenant by their bank. I have one account per each property and only one bank account. So all expenditures and income for a specific house are in one account. Every checkbook is placed in the property's folder. After receiving the deposit slip and rent, the mail teller of the bank credit the account of the property immediately and sends me a confirmation of deposit that includes the date and date, as well as the amount and the name of the bank on it by mail in my mailbox. The check is on its way to being cleared We have evidence from an independent third party to prove that you paid the rent in time (to receive the rent discount) or was not paid in time (tenant must pay the rent in full and any late charges in order to restore the the discounts on rent). The deposit slip of the bank reaches my office I post it to my checking account and pay off the mortgage. My record keeping ends for the month, unless there are any operational costs. Then I make a change to my spreadsheet (one sheet for each house, that has three columns with the 36 lines). Rents paid by month on line 1. Line 3 the page I write down the different expenses, and break them down over the month. After subtracting the monthly costs from the rent, my monthly net will be listed to line 36. My tax return is nearly done. Every house's income and expenses totals as well as the net are transferred to a monthly overview sheet that gives a comprehensive view.

Make use of any system that is simple for you to use. Install the system after you have purchased your first investment property. Do not do as I did and discover that you have seven apartment buildings, with no records-keeping system and three additional buildings that are under consideration for purchase. This is not the right time to determine that you need an organized system. It took me several months to organize my life since I didn't have a plan. If you are a computer enthusiast keep your data on it . Let me know how it goes.

Non-payment issues A tenant who has not paid rent would have liked to paid me had they had the cash. Once you've identified the reason the rent is not being paid and you have made a decision, it's now time for you. Every state has a process for expulsion. Certain are more efficient than others. Certain states appear to believe that a lease is a guarantee document. For instance, in the District of Columbia (where I have never been or will never be) in accordance with the laws of the legal system the eviction process could take up to thirteen months, if the tenant understands what he's doing. This is a one-o-n-g period with no rental revenue.

Additionally, you'll be able to enjoy the excitement of watching tenants who aren't paying rent slowly demolish the building. Five or four of these catastrophes can make the most difficult investor even if they have a large sum of money. Make sure to seek expert legal counsel before you require it. Eviction costs can be a nightmare. Find out what exactly the legal charges are and include the lost rent, time and effort. Look at the totality of these expenses and also consider the possibility of destruction of the property due to an angry tenant. The word "expensive" is a good description for it. There's a better solution.

Review the lease of your tenant who is not paying (any Guarantors?). Next, you should talk to them in-person. Be patient and listen to the responses. Don't threaten anyone, or you could get your deceit exposed. You can win by using sugar. The majority of the times they're just not able to afford the funds and would be happy to move to a smaller and less expensive home in the event that they could save up to cover one month's security, one month's rent and enough money to cover their moving costs. Combine these numbers to your mind. If the amount is less than the eviction process, you can offer to deposit the cash (cash) in an escrow in your lawyer's office. The cash will be his on when he's out (he's has three days) The property is cleaned up to the highest standards (subject to your approval and inspection) and keys are given the lawyer.

Reduced Management There are a variety ways to reduce management while still enjoying many of the advantages of real property. The first is to turn your property portfolio to a management company that is qualified. I've never tried this. Therefore I cannot be in a position to give you advice. It is sense to assume that nobody is concerned about the long-term health of an investment more than the investor. So, prior to giving your real estate assets with someone else conduct extensive investigation and research into the background and reputation of the manager you are considering. I'd like to know the number of houses that he owns and the length of time he's owned these properties.

In 1981 I was thinking that if tenants were also owner of the house, then they would be more careful and be more responsible in paying their rent on time. Thus, I decided to sell half my properties in the Raleigh region. Some of my tenants have were part of the plan. Most did not. If I found a vacant property, I put up ads in which I offered to let the house, sell the entire of the property or sell an ownership stake of 50. Then all vacant houses and newly purchased ones were added to the program. The years that followed I have never had any issues at all with my tenants or owners. Some have suggested that there may be serious issues when the tenant or owner ceases to pay. Therefore, be cautious as a guide. Once again, seek competent legal help. Here's my equity sharing plan.

I spoke to people who replied to my ads , allowing me to discuss the three options such as buying, renting shares of ownership. When they realized the advantages of the former, nearly everyone opted for the option. Because I owned ownership of the houses as trust, it proved straightforward to establish an agreement that would allow the new owner/tenant to purchase their share over a set amount of time. The monthly payments were one half of mortgage payments and one-half rent. They also assigned their lease for their one-half beneficial interest in exchange for security on their lease. In the event of a default, they ended their lease. The lease holder made monthly payments through the account designated for the lease established in an institution in the local area. This would create a clear account of the timing of the payments. The bank, with an unimportant service fee was able to make the each month mortgage repayments. I am taking my net monthly profits to cash a check to the account. To make tax-free, we divided the tax-deductible expenses.

Everyone was content. The owner/tenant was buying the home they would not be able to afford. They received more tax benefits than they could have gotten by renting. They were extremely driven to take care of and maintain their home . They were also motivated to pay their monthly bill earlier, as a part of every payment was creating equity, which was beneficial for them. They were aware that in the event they ever faced financial difficulties they could inform me that they were paying their monthly bills with the equity they had built up in their contract to earn an interest that was beneficial to them.

The contract I signed with the owner/tenant was in perpetuity. There was no obligation to buy-out from either party. If they decided to dispose of the home my name was first person they approached. The agreement required five valuations from five Realtors(r) selected by the owner/tenant. We organized opinions of value in ascending order, and then discarded the most expensive and lowest value. The three middle estimations of worth were then averaged and the result was what we call the "fair market value" of the property. The proportion of their share was determined by the amount of equity they'd built up or exhausted in their contract to get one-half in the interest they were entitled to. My contract was to buy the property in cash, or at their choice I would continue the process at their new residence.

I was very happy as I was able to make a passive investment that allowed me to rent double the amount of houses that had motivated owners or tenants. Additionally, my cash flow per home was in excess of $100 per month, which is more than if had rented the property outright. It was also possible to make all these transactions without having to put up any cash.

There are always issues with equity participation contracts. Be sure to plan them well and ensure that they are totally transparent in a way that all parties are aware the situation.

SHARE OWNERSHIP CONTINUES: A good my friend owns more than fifty percent of the houses with no management issues. He receives an annual report and a net check each year for each property from different co-owners or managers. When he comes across an "good" deal, he arranges the transaction and arranges it for his preferred local manager. After all documents are completed, sealed and signed then he's on his way to a new deal. It could be a worthwhile objective that is worth taking on.

Another option is to sell at a significant discount (with an option to buy back in the event of a 10 months) one or several of your investment homes to a trusted acquaintance who has a lot of homes and has a savvy manager. As long as you've got an authenticated "notice of agreement" to the home, the deal is protected and you can move on to other offers for ten years and in order to buy back the property at a mutually agreed strike price. There are many ways to structure the transaction based on your specific requirements as well as those of your trusted partner.

Whatever you require from managing your real estate Always strive to master new and more effective methods. There are many knowledgeable seminar instructors eager to discuss their knowledge with you. Your views on hands-on management could change over the passage of time, so it's good to have alternatives.

Chapter 13: Do I Purchase Residential or commercial Real Estate?

What's the best investment plan for you? Do you want to invest in commercial or residential real estate? These are important questions that require some thinking and consideration. However, before you are able to answer these questions, you have be aware of the differences between these different investment options.

The term "residential real estate" is usually described as homes with a single family according to the majority of experts. Real estate that is residential is a distinct benefit. Let's take a look at the benefits of investing in residential real estate.

The main benefit is that all people in the world require protection from the elements in order to live. With this in mind the fact that the residential property market is not subject to technological advancements. There isn't a technological breakthrough or invention that would render the human requirement of shelter obsolete. Humanity's survival depends on residential real estate. This is why it's one of the most secure investments available. Real estate for residential purposes is a well-tested investment from the start of the time. Let's now look at commercial real property.

Real estate for commercial use is thought of by the majority of people as property used for commercial use. What exactly does this mean? Maybe I can clarify that with a few examples. Commercial real estate includes buildings or land such as shopping malls gas stations, office parks and car washes, restaurants and hotels, among others. What is the most significant benefit from commercial property?

The biggest benefit is leases that last for a long time. If Taco Bell leases your commercial property and your business is successful, barring a unexpected event, you should be able to retain the tenant for a long time for as long as the company continues to flourish and expand. Companies typically negotiate rent increases automatically as time passes in the lease, too. These companies understand that the importance of location and are keen to keep the owners of their properties content. We've talked about commercial and residential real estate, but we've missed one crucial type of property: Multi-family real estate. What exactly is multi-family real estate? What is the asset class does multifamily real estate belong to?

Multi-family real estate includes duplexes and apartment structures. It's simply a building that is occupied by several families. I classify multi-family homes as commercial, not residential, and will explain why. Single-family real estate encourages long-term tenant occupancy. The layout and design of these structures is the main driver. A house is constructed to accommodate one family. There are outdoor spaces for recreation, such as front and back yards. These are often quaint however they are private. Tenants are generally more comfortable in homes with a single family. Apartments have a distinct style.

Apartment buildings require minimal space to make the most profit. The structure itself is constructed to maximize efficiency. Small bathrooms, tiny rooms that can accommodate multiple families under one shared roof. After having lived in apartments throughout my life, I'm convinced that many people think of them as a short-term solution for their housing needs. Apartments are noisy, cramped, with less privacy. Tenants move in and out of these apartments. If there is the option there are a few who would opt for an apartment that is suitable for their long-term living needs. Apartments are akin to motels for me, and I'd guess that many people would are in agreement with my opinion. I categorize apartment buildings in similar to the way I classify motels : commercial property.

We now know the distinction between residential and commercial real estate, it is time to consider the most important issues of all. Which one is superior? Which one should I go with?

The answer is both.

Residential real estate can be an excellent investment when purchased at the best cost. Real estate in residential areas typically draws families, and families are more likely to remain in their homes for longer. Families tend to be reluctant to remove children from school and their friends therefore expect long-term leases for these kinds of structures. However, not everything is perfect when it comes to residential real property. The majority of the time residential real estate generates less profits than commercial property. The majority of people who invest in residential real estate are disappointed and demoralized after long periods with negative money flow. Does this mean that you should not invest in residential real estate? No, no, absolutely not. But, it is important to buy these properties at a reasonable cost and be prepared for a lower income after expenditures.

Do you require a substantial positive cash flow right now? If yes, then you may want to consider commercial real property. The majority of people enter commercial real estate through the purchase of the building. I'll need to talk about the advantages and disadvantages of these buildings.

Apartment buildings can generate positive cash flow, if you have the structure completely filled. If you are able to make it so. If the majority of people have a choice they'll choose a house over an apartment all the time. Humans are social creatures, however, they also love privacy. There's no real private space in an apartment. If you manage to find tenants, don't count on them to remain for all the time. Apartment buildings are not permanent solutions to one's longer-term housing requirements. Once they're financially stable, they're likely to purchase a home. What's the most effective strategy for apartment buildings? Find the market that is likely to stay in the house for a prolonged period. It is usually low income those who receive government vouchers. The housing options they have are limited because a large portion of property owners are reluctant to accept vouchers from the government because of bureaucratic red tape and an negative stigma attached to government vouchers and their beneficiaries. In the event that they do they are tenants, they will probably remain for a while and lower the vacancy rate and turnover.

This leads us to our original question. What asset class is the best? Should I invest in commercial or residential real estate? There are many types of real estate to spread the risk. As with all markets that are subject to fluctuations, the real estate market is depending on the current economic situation. In certain times, residential real estate is hot. At other times the residential real estate market will have a colder temperature than middle of a microwave-cooked burrito. A portfolio of various real estate properties will even out your portfolio and reduce the risk. If your home isn't being rented, it's likely that it's your building taking the gaps. If your apartment isn't doing well, perhaps the rent you receive from the restaurant owner who rents the property along Main Street will. Similar to stocks, diversification can save you from losing everything. In real estate, diversity works in the same manner. When you begin to build your real estate empire, make sure that you diversify into other asset classes in real estate. I haven't met a single person who has made it a habit to achieve success by placing all their eggs into one basket.

Chapter 14: Stock Market Investing

Questions Answered

Are there any proofs that I'll make money from investing in stocks?

Based on information through Standard and Poors, the returns on stocks from 1926 between 1926 and 2013. The average return was 9.9 percent. Although this implies that you can certainly earn money from when investing on stocks, the data does not consider the potential risk involved. There is no guarantee of whether the stock you choose will provide an income on your investment, particularly if you are an investor who is yet to master the basics. The higher risk comes with the greater chance of a reward it is important to create an efficient plan and stick to it, you're more likely to be better in the end.

What are the best methods to determine if a stock is healthy?

While the precise metrics that determine whether you should buy a stock will differ based on the strategy for investing in stocks that you decide to use, you're always required to look at the quarterly earnings reports that every publicly traded company has to provide to the Securities and Exchange Commission (SEC). In the first place, you're going be looking at the ratio of P/E, earnings per share as well as the price/book ratio, which indicates the amount shareholders are willing to pay in comparison to the stated value of the business.

How can I locate analyst opinions on an individual stock?

While it is essential to conduct your own research in accordance with the strategy for trading you've selected, you'll be interested in what experts have to say particularly when you're the first to begin. The research of well-known analysts can be found on the internet through sites like Finance.Yahoo.com, Zacks.com and MorningStar.com. In addition, if you're working with a full-service brokerage company, they usually offer analyst suggestions and recommendations.

Furthermore, Zacks.com provides a record of different analyst's performance rates.

How do I purchase an IPO?

A lot of IPOs aren't open to everyone and are restricted to those who are serious about investing. To determine whether a particular IPO is accessible to you, you'll be required to look up its SEC registration and check the section that deals with underwriting. This will give you information on the financial institutions that are participating in the IPO of interest. Then, you can take this information and utilize it to locate an agent who is associated with one of these institutions and inquire about an IPO directly.

What does shorting stock mean?

If an investor decides to short the stock, what happens is that they will more than a little borrow an amount of the shares from the brokerage, and then sell it to a buyer because they believe its current value is undervalued. If the price falls and the person who sold it earns money from the difference between what it was sold for and also on the amount they must pay after the price drops. The ability to short stocks is only available when the brokerage you use permits trading in margin. This means you can trade more than you have actually in your account for trading.

What is an acceptable return for a beginner investor?

Since the beginning of 1900 in the 1900s, in the early 1900s, stocks market has experienced an average return of around 10 percent. When inflation is taken into consideration it is possible to witness your investment grow by a factor of approximately 10 years. It doesn't mean that you're always earning 10% annually but it's an average. But, the amount is highly debated by financial experts. In the conservative sense, the rate you could anticipate is thought by experts to range between 7 to 8 percent.

Do I need to put my money into an hedge fund?

The majority of hedge funds have investments in multiple areas other than stocks. Some of them aren't controlled by the SEC making it hard to know what their worth is, or to assure their liquidity. In addition, they're generally only available to what are referred to as accredited investors, which are those who have an asset worth over one million dollars at the time they purchase into the fund or who earn over 200,000 bucks each year. In all, they're not a suitable option for beginners to invest in.

Should I invest in ETFs? (ETF)?

Exchange-traded funds offer the same flexibility as stocks and the lower costs associated with mutual funds. Contrary to mutual funds they are mainly focused on indexes of stocks. That means that their prices are constantly changing and you have the option to sell them at anytime. There are numerous kinds of ETFs, it's crucial to know the ETF you're looking at the purpose of it, and how they align with your financial goals. If you own a substantial IRA that will grow or have an enormous amount of money you want to invest, an ETF could be a great alternative, however, if you don't, then you're likely to need to look at different alternatives.

Why do companies offer shares?

Stocks are issued by companies to get an inflow of capital. This amount they receive will depend on the quantity of shares that they offer and the they value each share are worth. This is how the business makes use of this money to expand their business without worrying about returning the funds just like they would through the loan. If the company succeeds, they may be able to purchase back their shares or issue additional shares in order to capitalize on the success of their business.

What is the tax treatment of stocks?

Capital gains on investments in stocks can be taxed 15 percent when you keep a stock for more than a year. If you decide to sell the stock within a shorter period than that , any gain you earn is instead an investment that is short-term in nature and, therefore it is taxed as all your other income is. Dividends are generally subject to tax at 15 percent when they are held for a certain amount of time after the dividend last paid , which is usually approximately two months.

Chapter 15: The Calculation of Cash Flow

Although you might already have an idea of the amount of money you will need to buy the property and renovating it, when you begin the search for the right property you will need a more realistic and sensible budget is what you must make right now. The first step is to establish a rough idea of the cost of the house you plan to purchase. In order to do this, use property comps. Property comps is a technique that focuses on the prices of other properties within the same region with similar numbers of bedrooms, kitchens restrooms, car parks, and washrooms. It is a simple way to could refer to it as a comparative look at the cost of property by gathering information about the cost that similar houses have. For comps on property it is possible to get in touch with the real estate agents in the region in which you plan to purchase the property.

It is recommended to get in touch with more than one agent to obtain an accurate estimate.

The next step to complete is to establish an idea of the cost of renovation. The price of renovations often is more expensive than you imagined at the beginning. This is a problem that a majority of real estate investors have to face when flipping their home and an incorrect estimate can lead them in a position that is not salvageable. It is important to be cautious in estimating the costs for repair of the property. However, it's quite simple if you pay an effort with care and care. Start by writing down the locations and items you believe require repair or replaced in your home. Make it more thorough by listing the items or materials you have to purchase, and also the amount of material. Visit the market and ask on the cost of the material. It is best to visit wholesale stores or markets in order to purchase the material for less than the market price. In addition to exploring for bargains in the market it is also possible to make contact with a few contractors. It would be extremely beneficial to locate a contractor through your circle of friends, even if you are able to solicit any contractor's services and then pay the contractor in exchange for his consultation services. Then, show the contractor the home you've selected and request an estimate of what it will cost. Because contractors perform this on a daily basis, they can give you a more accurate picture since he is able to observe the tasks that need to be completed that are not apparent.

After you have a general concept of the cost of renovation then you can estimate the amount you're likely to receive to purchase the house. The final estimation of cash you receive should include the value of the home, the cost of renovation (including materials and labor) and the expense of paperwork and include some money to cover the difficulties you might encounter when you are remodeling the home.

Reduce Charges

When you've calculated the amount you'll need, you're now required to make arrangements for cash. If you don't have money in your account There are numerous alternatives to get cash. You can opt for a home loans from banks. A majority of banks will offer only a tiny amount of money for homes that are not furnished but you should speak to bank representatives to find the best deal. If you don't obtain a bank loan in the first , you may consider a "Hard loans". The loan is provided by individuals or companies that are prepared to take on risky ventures such as flipping houses. Find the companies or individuals that are within your local area, and submit your proposal and receive the loan. Be aware that lenders who grant loans to hard borrowers do so or loans with a higher interest rate or with a less mature date. If you've determined your earnings and returns through this type of investment, this shouldn't cause you to worry. You could provide them with the rate of interest and the maturity date of the loan taking into consideration your expectations for earnings. Hard loans are considered to be the best option for most real estate investors who invest in house flips because it is likely that you will receive the huge amount of money needed for the entire process from the hard-loan lenders.

There are various opportunities you can take advantage of when organizing cash. It is possible to find loaners through your contacts. If you know someone willing to offer you a money at a fair rate of interest, take advantage of it. Let them know how much you're committed and driven to take on this endeavor and how they will profit from the project. Another option is to take out a "Home Equity Loan" that can be used with the purchase price of your home. You could finance the home you recently purchased and take out a loan against it. There are also privately-owned investors that are ready to take on these kinds of businesses. Whatever you decide to do your credit score will play an important role in securing an loan. Make sure to review your credit report to improve its appeal to those who are seeking loans.

In essence, I would suggest that the right mixture of all of these options will provide you with not just the amount for home flipping, but also peace of mind to you , and you'll be able focus on re-selling and renovation.

Renovations: Begin With Instant Repairs

The next step in your process of flipping houses is to make the house more attractive. This is the most crucial aspect of the whole process. the way you remodel your house will determine the future value of your home. When you decide to do the remodeling, you'll find yourself you are asking yourself questions such as Where do you begin? What's the most important thing? What is the time frame required? Etc. The initial four steps took about 10 days, and then you're left with 20 days to remodel and sell the property. This means you have about 15 days to make improvements to the house. The remaining 5 days are reserved to sell the house. To finish all the tasks involved in renovation on time, you must to create a timetable. Prioritize your work and establish the time frame for each job.

Prior to that, you must identify the issues that need to be resolved promptly. The plumbing issues and electricity, as well as air conditioners and heaters must be dealt with first since they might require some structural repairs and you might need to install pipes that will not be completed until you have repaired the roof and floors, or will take additional time and expense to fix them later. The next step is to determine if repairs are required for doors or windows. If you notice any breaks or cracks, take steps to repair them and then polish them to give them the appearance of new. If repairs don't suffice to be considered, you might have to purchase new floors. It is the next thing to do fixing the issues with flooring or the roof. Be smart and if you have the money to allow you to, consider buying carpets that are brand new instead of opting for a brand new floor or tiles which will cost more. When you are renovating your home is a possibility, you could also participate in this process by completing a lot of labor intensive work on your own. This will not only help you save time and money but also give you an insider's view of the process of renovation that will aid you not just with the present project but can be extremely useful for future projects. Remember that the knowledge you gain from firsthand experience you acquire is superior to any expert's advice. In your first endeavor, aside from enlisting the help of other people, you should complete as many researches and do as much work yourself as much as you can.

A common mistake committed by a majority of real property investors is to focus more on bedrooms and living areas and thus have a small money left over for kitchens and bathroom. When you prioritize your work of remodeling, don't forget to set aside some extra cash to renovate kitchens and bathrooms, since it will earn you additional bonus points when you'll be selling the property.

After you have finished working on the inside of the home, focus your attention to an area for parking, the garage area or a lawn in front of the home. This area of the property can be more dirty than other areas. However, it's surprising that it does not cost more than it might appear. The main reason is that it is more prone to cleaning than repair. A thorough cleaning and fresh paint can do wonders to help you with the outside area of the home.

One method of saving money while renovating is to solicit assistance from your family and friends family members. It can be fun to renovate in the presence of your family or friends and will save you amount of time and money.

Chapter 16: To Manage Yourself or Property Manage

Self-managed properties are defined as a property in which the owner is in charge of all aspects. While the hiring of a property management firm is when the property manager handles all day-today tasks and is kind of an "in between" between tenants and owner. Certain owners prefer to take on some of the duties, while the property management company doing the remaining tasks. Others would prefer the property management firm to handle everything.

We've noticed that many property owners prefer to manage their own properties themselves. This is great, but be aware that you will be available to address any concerns with the tenants who are contacting you directly. Based on the tenant, they may not respect your time as well as they ought to. It's always ideal to establish boundaries in the beginning (usually in the lease's do's and do's and) However, even so, it could be a challenge.

What is the best option for you? There are occasions where the choice is simple to make. The property may not be located in your area or be too distant to manage effectively. If you're unable in collecting rent, manage repairs, or be present in case of emergencies or other emergencies, etc. The most effective option could be to hire an estate management company.

Other possibilities include the ones where the property may be too big. The business is new and assuming the responsibility of a 60 to 100-unit apartment complex could be a challenge. It's not easy, and one can envision the strain this could cause.

There may be instances when you simply do not have the expertise necessary. You can certainly hire other people to do specific tasks, but it could be costly. Consider which options you have and decide in the early stages before burning out occurs. I'm sure it can happen when you're not set up correctly.

Let's take it further to help you decide. Some advantages of a self-managed homes are:

The savings and the profits are yours - yay! Management companies vary on what they want in return, but the majority of them want the percentage of deposits, rent etc.

Greater control - You'll be able to better understand the happenings on your property , and you will be able to quickly take decisions based on this. The knowledge gained is effective.

A great experience, especially at the beginning, when controlling yourself, you will gain lots of experience on how everything functions. This will be invaluable later on when you expand your units.

Residential property managers serve as a barrier between owner and tenant, with direct communication being restricted. In some instances the property owner does not have interaction with tenants;. They only speak to their property management firm. A property management firm discovers tenants, handles any repairs or issues as well as collects rents and covers the costs (if the owner desires this kind of service).

There are many advantages for a management firm that include:

They're set up to manage residential rental properties and already have everything needed to be in the place, or near it, including necessary documents. At first you may not have a office or staff, but the property management company has one.

This saves time - It's clear that if you have someone else managing the day-to-day business operations You are now free to pursue at a full-time job should you wish, search for alternative investments, or simply take advantage of more time. You'll feel relaxed knowing the knowledge that they are knowledgeable and can take charge of everything for you. Priceless!

A lesser amount of stress - You'll be dealing with tenants who are easy to manage, and others who will test to test your nerves. The help of a property management firm to handle that extra stress frees you to run your business, including finding new rentals.

If your property exceeds an amount of units as required by law, you must to have a property manager present on the premises.

The company that manages your property is more knowledgeable about the laws and procedures of your particular state, which could be very advantageous. Apart from the usual guidelines, other things to take into consideration include how much deposit you are able to request and the rules for inspections, and so on.

In my location, the laws governing tenants change every year. Property management companies stay at the forefront of all changes so that I don't have to be concerned. Owners who don't use an agency for property management may not be current with all the latest laws, which could lead to issues.

A building that has more than 16 units is legally required to have a property manager who lives within the building in my region of California. If the landlord wishes to manage this large of building, it must employ an on-site manager, as required by law.

It is also important to note that it is crucial to study the laws and codes of the government in your region that deal with the management of your property. There are laws regarding security and insurance, taxes and so on. That you may not know about.

Some states, like California as well as other states, also have property management requirements that require them to have the license of a real estate broker as well as be employed by someone with. Furthermore, ongoing education and licensure could be required. Discuss this with the business you're considering hiring as well as doing your own research, or speaking with experts.

Chapter 17: Zoning Violations

Local government (not government officials) as well as their boards of planning are responsible for budgeting, review of site plans as well as building code. The zoning of a property may be located in any areas:

Residential

Commercial

Industrial

Land that is vacant (unimproved)

Agricultural

Public spaces that are open to the public

Parklands (recreational areas managed by the state or local government)

Recreation areas

Institutional Hospitals, jails, prisons and courthouses, colleges, campuses as well as public school.

Residential zoning applies to multi-family and single-family homes. A single-family home may be allowed to include an additional use, such as an outbuilding or a mother-in law suite, and it is also permitted to have a home occupation (i.e. work at the home). Homeowners who live in an area that is down-zoned and believe that downzoning (changing the zoning) has damaged the value of their property can seek reverse condemnation (for compensation).

Bulk Zoning controls also created by local government through local ordinances regulate the density (number of inhabitants for each sq ft) as well as volume (amount of construction per square foot) within an area. There are some restrictions which can be imposed on any neighborhood and the properties that are part of it like:

FAR, also known as floor-to-area ratio where floor is all square feet, and area is that total amount of area surrounding the property. Suburbia can have a FAR close or below 1 , while downtown has a larger FAR, 7-15, allowing for greater density. FAR only covers those areas that are inhabited, therefore parking isn't included in the measure (you can imagine what an empty parking space has an FAR of 0).

Area per unit of lot Municipalities may set the minimum square footage for each unit in order to restrict density in the same way as FAR. Unit here means the floors or units that are stacked. If a property has an unbalanced multiple of the unit's Lot area then there is likely to be vacant space. For instance If the area of the property has a size of 5000 sq. feet, and each unit's Lot size is expected by law to exceed 1500 sq. feet the developer will only be able to create 3 units to 4500 square feet. This leaves 500 square feet that are undeveloped.

Maximum Building Height limit the building's height and, consequently, its size relative to the space.

Setbacks: back, front or side setbacks establish the minimum distance between a structure and its property line , and also help reduce the bulk.

Open space restrictions on site This applies to multi-unit structures and the amount of open , usable outdoor space a structure must offer its residents

Zoning Actions and Variances are local regulations that govern the changing of the zoning allowances. Moratoriums prevent construction projects. For example, if schools are overcrowded, a ban is put in place until a new school is constructed or the existing school expands in size. To request a variance to the zoning ordinance homeowner has to apply to the appeals board for zoning (within the plan board) to be approved.

The Use Variance necessary to amend the zoning ordinance , for example changing it from commercial to residential. To be able to do this homeowners must demonstrate that:

The economic benefit is not realized due to the existing Zoning.

The Hardship property is unique in its property.

It is not self-inflicted.

The changes will not impact the other residents of the area.

A Area Variance is required to modify the bulk zoning control. In order to get approval, one needs to prove that:

The changes won't affect other properties within the neighborhood.

The transformation cannot be accomplished via any other method

This isn't an important change

A Special Use Permit (aka conditional permits) is the permit to construct something that is for the benefit of the public even if it's not in compliance with Zoning laws, like the golf course that is located in the residential zone. However it is a non-conforming use in the event that after rezoning, properties that aren't in compliance are considered grandfathered in. If, however, the same property is sold later to a new owner, they must be in compliance with the new Zoning Ordinance. This is an issue with the title that will be found prior to closing.

Final TALLY of CLOSING Costs

Zillow and other well-known websites estimate closing costs ranging from 2 to 5% of the selling price! When you are looking at closing costs, be aware that your lender could need you to pay for up to one year of property taxes and insurance (including flood insurance, if it's required) and HOA charges.

Let's look at a list on closing expenses for a typical home that is 1500-2000 square feet in a that ranges from $250,000 to $500,000.

Home Inspection $300-$500.

Survey inspection (if needed) Cost varies between $250 and $1,000.

Title Insurance $1500-$1000.

Might or might exclude the costs of the search for a title search ($200-400).

Settlement fee payable by the company that holds title, or escrow agent Amount: $500.

It usually costs around $2 per $1000 in the sale cost.

The fee for loan origination by the lender is 0.5-1.5 points (or percent of the sale price).

It could be that they do not include fees for loan applications ($300) or credit score ($25) or Flood monitoring and certification ($50).

A loan discount fee (optional) As much as 5 percent (or five points) of the purchase price could be paid in advance to reduce the rate of interest over the term of the loan.

Appraisal (if required by the lender) (if required by lender): $250-$500.

Recording Fee $100.

Transfer Tax: varies considerably. It could be zero as in Texas and a flat fee like Arizona's 20-dollar per month flat rate, or even as much as 3% of the house price, such as in Delaware. Most states have 0.5 percent or less. However, you should check with the state you reside in.

Other possible costs that can be negotiated may include:

* Septic or Plumber Sewer Inspection: $100 to $300.

*Well Water Test: $100-$300. It is required on properties in rural areas that are not connected to an major water source.

* Gas Line Leak Inspection: $100-300.

* Radon Inspection Home Testing: $15 for kits and $100-150 for an expert inspection.

* Pest and Termite Inspection: $50 to $150.

* Lead Paint Inspection: $300-$500.
* Roof inspection: $100 to $150; fairly inexpensive if the home inspectors discover a problem with your roof, which could uncover thousands of dollars in repairs an inspection.

Over 50% of homeowners are shocked by the high cost of closing expenses. You may spend months or years, saving up to pay for a down payment, but never realize that you may pay more in closing costs than you paid in the downpayment! This has always irked me. Agents are at risk in the process of negotiating with sellers and buyers not knowing if buyers are able to manage to pay for greater than down payments, and the sellers are willing contribute to the higher cost of closing.

However, Concise Reads scholar know that it is important to prepare. You should expect between one and a half percent (or less) of the selling value of the property for the form of prepayments (property taxes , insurance and other costs for at minimum 12 months) as well as another 2-

5% of the price for sale in closing expenses. This is an additional 36 percent of the cost, which is in along with the initial down payment, and not including the commission of the broker, which is 6% that we're expecting the seller to pay as well as the 0.5 percent mortgage insurance, assuming you make the minimum down amount.

Let's take a look at an example.

For a home valued at $500,000 and a conventional loan that has a 20 percent down payment, you're contemplating a total of $100,000 as a down payment, and an additional $15,000 to $30,000. in closing expenses and prepayment. You can find an institution that permits the borrower to pay a lower down payment, or the government-backed loan however, the closing costs won't change. If the majority of home buyers are at the table to finalize the deal, many realize they aren't able to afford closing on the property. After all, you've put in enough time in search of the ideal home that the only way to get it is to get the seller to pay for a portion of the expenses (they do not have to, and won't do so in an auction market) If you want to request that the lender pay for the cost, but charge you more interest and then go to your retirement account (up of $10,000) or ask your family members to give you money to help you close the deal.

Prepare yourself to cover closing costs. This is buying a smaller house that is within the budget. Keep in mind Rich Dad Poor Dad's lesson your house (if it isn't used to earn money) can be a risk and you should minimize the risk. The thing that new homebuyers do not realize is that the costs aren't over once you have purchased an apartment. It's possible to set aside 2 percent of the purchase price in a separate bank account every year to cover repairs or maintenance. That's an average of around $10,000 per year for a home worth $500,000 during the term that the loan. In addition, the major expense that you incur when you go from a tenant to becoming a homeowner is the "stuff" you need to purchase, such as new garage door openers, new or used lawn mower, lights fixtures, furniture and fixtures - the list is endless. You must budget for those costs as well. The thing you'll see soon is that, if you take into account all the expenses of purchasing an entire new house then you'll be more comfortable by a house that's at a minimum 3X or less your annual taxable income. This may seem like I'm destroying your hopes, but in time, you'll realize that it's financially sensible. If you have $100,000 of tax-deductible earnings, you should think twice about purchasing a home which is priced higher than $300,000. For more reasons why this would make sense, you should take note of the details I share about taxes on property next.

Property taxes make up greater than one-third of the local government revenues, so they're definitely not likely to disappear anytime in the near future. Taxes on property differ from state to state, as well as by county or city as smaller local governments also have property tax rates. Louisiana is the state with the least property taxes, at 0.18 percent, while New Jersey has the highest property tax at 1.89 percent. States earn revenue through income tax, sales tax, corporate tax and property tax in addition to other charges for the majority of services offered by state. If a state advertises the possibility of a tax reduction in one of these tax categories, it is likely that they will find an opportunity to pay the difference by reducing any of other types of taxes. State administration is like a company, and requires funds to run. If a state gives large tax break for companies the reason is that they wish to collect tax from the greater personal income tax of new employees moving into the state. If a city or county provides tax relief, such as Philadelphia which provides 10 year tax breaks on property taxes for new construction projects, then they are making profits elsewhere.

In the instance of Philadelphia the tax is an 8 sales tax of 8%, and an income tax of 7% for non-residents and residents who reside in Philadelphia however reside in

Delaware for instance in addition to the 10% corporate income tax. The thing that is interesting about Philadelphia is that many economists believe that the reason they choose to tax, and not tax, is not well thought-out. It turns out that most workers are renters, and the majority of retired people are homeowners. The higher income and sales tax has driven people to Philadelphia and the increase in Philadelphia employees is similar to the urban cities such as Baltimore or Detroit.

Alabama along with Louisiana have one of the lowest property taxes of any state, with 0.33 percent and 0.18 percent, respectively. However, their sales taxes are among one of the largest in the nation at 10% and 9% respectively. Texas which is a non-income tax state has property taxes of 1.81 percent! If you earn $100,000 in tax-deductible income and buy an apartment with a purchase cost of $500,000 Texas the property tax would be $9000 in property tax , or almost the same as the state's income tax , if there was any property tax!

Homebuyers who are new to the market purchase properties that are multiples of their annual tax-deductible income. The lender's requirement for an income to debt ratio of 25% for housing percentage of 25% implies that they'll allow you to pay 25 percent of your taxable income (assuming that you do not have any other debts) for the mortgage. For a person with $100,000 of tax-deductible income, $25,000 in mortgage annual payments at an average rate of interest and 30-year terms give an amount of $440,000 in loan. With that they pay 20% down is possible, they can afford the home worth $550,000, or 5.5X of the annual income. This means more money for states with the highest property tax. If you'd like to avail the benefits of states that do not have income tax that has a higher property tax ensure that your property isn't greater than 3 times your annual tax-deductible income. This way, you will make a profit from the financial engineering that was created by States' governments.

Chapter 18: Property For Taxes

You've probably heard of buying a house for what is due on tax owed back. If you fail to pay your tax and the bank fails to intervene and settle the tax then the mortgage gets erased.

Let's say that you have a mortgage that is first for $200,000, but you haven't paid taxes. The government is likely to pursue your property. The standard is that the government will always get its money, especially when property is involved. Banks could be completely wiped out, but rest assuredthat the government will search for the property to collect the tax revenue. What they'll do is to auction the property to pay tax back owed at the top bidder, in the majority of instances.

Tax Deeds

In this chapter, I'll teach you on Tax Deeds. There will always be those who do not pay their property taxes. They do not want to pay taxes, it's just that they don't have the money, or you me, the tax obligations were simply not paid. It could be that the property was acquired and the heirs didn't pay attention to the specifics and the property is then sold for the amount of tax due. If property taxes remain unpaid, the property is sold to a buyer who will pay the tax owed.

Check out examples that are from this month, and not the same as what was happening some time ago.

Real Exemple #1:

I have a property that has the assessed price of $230,000 however, the initial bid is just $22,000. This means that the taxes due back are $22,000. As you could imagine the tax back was paid at the last minute. This is known as "REDEEMED," the property was redeemed to pay back the taxes, meaning that the taxes were paid prior to the property being sold at auction , thus the term "redeemed.

There's no way to change this, but the great part is that it will be exchanged before the auction begins. It's not like when you bid and you're just so happy since you've have won the property, but later you realize you're not going to get it. The property will likely be exchanged prior to the auction starts and that's the great news. If the property you're interested about is cleared, you'll be able to go on to the next offer.

Real Exemple #2:

In this instance, a person could purchase the property located in Fort Myers for $3,900 thru an auction of tax deeds, not a long time ago, but this month! It's current at the date of this article. It's now on a Tuesday at 6:00 pm in Lee County, Florida.

Someone bought this house for $3900. This is true. Someone paid $3,900 to purchase the property at Fort Myers, Florida using this exact strategy.

It's actually a home. At first I thought that it was expensive because it was so inexpensive. I can't think of one person who would be willing to buy a home with a house upon it, for $3900. This is a house with dirt underneath it. What do I pay attention to the state of the house?

You may be thinking, "Mike, but what do you do if it's rubbish. I'm talking about garbage." I'll take the item for 3,900 dollars. Why?

It's still a structure that has dirt beneath it. Someone is going to tackle that task. There's a person who would be willing to offer the buyer $12,000 or $13,000 or $14,000 to buy a house located in South Florida even if it's an immense fixer upper. The $3,900 house in this example might be in a terrible area, but it's located situated in Fort Myers, Florida. What is the worst thing that could happen? Don't forget that the majority of people don't have the money to buy these kinds of houses, because they lack the methods or tools I'm teaching you.

I don't care about how ugly it looks. If you bought it for $3,900 it and claimed that you would sell it at an unprofitable price, I'd inquire about why you didn't make use of one of my strategies to sell your house online. Be aware that the majority of people do not have the capacity to purchase a house for less than $10,000, because I didn't train them.

However many times you try this, you'll come across amazing deals that will blow your out of the water! It's not like every deal is a hit. What I'm saying is there are deals available every day when you are aware of the right place to search. Perhaps you're thinking, "Mike, that's a extremely extreme illustration."

Yes, you won't be able to win when you don't participate.

The examples I'm studying in the study guide I came across today... today, the very day I'm writing this chapter. I'm not making them up. I'm not going say that these deals simply happen to you. I invest 30 to 40 minutes each day researching auctions for properties and I'm always well-prepared. I train people on how to organize their research.

For the sake of being clearYou won't usually find large extravagant, costly, incredible properties and buy the property for just $10,000. Someone will have to pay off the back taxes (redeem it) in the event that it's the most ridiculous offer. However, sometimes deals pass through the cracks. It's important to be part of this game in order to make.

One thing I can assure you of... If you claim, "I will never get the property. I'm not even going to submit a bid." You'll never be able to get the property. This is a guarantee. It all depends on your attitude.

When you've completed your homework and believe in this property, why not make bids? It's not expensive a cent to place a bid.

Conclusion

Now you are aware of the facts regarding motivated buyers. When you're watching a real estate expert go over and over about how much you could make buying houses from motivated sellers , and flipping them, remember the information you learned from this publication. I encourage you to be vigilant and take care to protect yourself. The people who are facing foreclosure are usually scared to death and are trying to hide that. Imagine your most hated family member and imagine that you have to surrender your pride and beg him to allow you to stay the couch few minutes. How humiliating could that be? The owners of homes that are abandoned and vacant are often irritated because they are constantly receiving low-ball offers to buy. They do not have the funds they require to put in the effort to repair the home, however they are aware of what the home across the street was is worth and they'd like the same amount of money for their home. Motivated sellers aren't always rational and frightening so be wary.